Y0-AGH-798

No Longer the Property of NOLS

910.4 W
Wilcox, L.A.
    Anson's voyage

66628

X

SEP 2 7 1995

OCT 3 0 1995

MAY   1 1993

OCT 0 7 1994

JUN 1 0 1996

NOV 2 6 1996

JUN 0 3 1998

MAR 1 8 1995

MAY 2 4 1995

JUN 2 1 1995

AUG 0 3 1995

Sequim - new

aw

**CLALLAM COUNTY LIBRARY**
HZ 2210 South Peabody Street
**PORT ANGELES, WASHINGTON 98362**

PRINTED IN U.S.A.

# Anson's Voyage

# ANSON'S VOYAGE

Written and Illustrated by

## L. A. WILCOX R.I., R.S.M.A.

CLALLAM COUNTY LIBRARY

ST. MARTIN'S PRESS: NEW YORK

66628

Copyright © 1970 by
G. BELL AND SONS, LTD

All rights reserved. For information write:
St. Martin's Press, Inc., 175 Fifth Avenue, New York, N.Y. 10010

First published in the United States of America in 1970

Library of Congress Catalog Card No.: 73-125589

AFFILIATED PUBLISHERS: Macmillan & Company, Ltd., London
also at Bombay, Calcutta, Madras and Melbourne
The Macmillan Company of Canada, Limited, Toronto

*Printed in Great Britain*

# Contents

# Illustrations

# Introduction

THIS IS the story of one of the great voyages round the world. It was made by a Naval commander who was hardly known to the British people when he set out, yet who by his great abilities and indomitable courage completed an epic chapter in our history and covered himself with glory. The voyage was undertaken for political reasons, a practical demonstration of national belligerence justified in the minds of the people by the infringement of their 'rights' in the New World. John Bull—Mr. Arbuthnot's newly cartooned typical Englishman—was not to be pushed aside by any damned foreigner.

History is, of course, full of instances of a like nature. Wars have been engendered by national pride demanding redress for insults, sustained or imagined. Governments have not hesitated to play on the emotions of peoples when improved trade and profits would result from military victory: and merchants, desirous of expanding their markets and sources of supply, have at various times managed to find men and money for pioneering expeditions into unknown countries. The fact that privation and hardship, and possibly death at the hands of hostile natives or enemy settlers might be their lot, does not seem to have deterred them in any way.

When monarchs took an interest and sponsored such a voyage, the ship sailed under the protection of the Crown and, having a better armament, could achieve greater success when force was required— and few such enterprises were completed without bloodshed. Governments naturally took great interest not only in their own world voyages and explorations but to a very great extent in those of other nations. Those same merchants also displayed no little anxiety when their foreign rivals circumnavigated the globe. All this is very easily understood by us, seeing that exactly the same national and mercantile interest and curiosity function today.

No voyaging of modern times has excited such concentrated attention as the present-day manned spacecraft journeys. In the same way, although they lacked the rapid communications that we enjoy, our forefathers wasted no time in acquiring the best reports of the great adventurers of their age. So it is not surprising that in the first edition of the book of Anson's Voyage there is a list of 1,826 subscribers who paid their money in advance in order to ensure a copy of the official account of an expedition to the other side of the world from one Englishman who had wiped Spain's eye. I have a copy of this first edition, on the flyleaf of which the purchaser has given his name which I had great pleasure in discovering in the list.

The title page of the book names as the author Richard Walter, the chaplain of the *Centurion*, but recent research has revealed that he was not solely responsible for this, the authorised story. Walter had access to officers' journals and it was generally understood that he would write the eagerly awaited history of Anson's great journey. However, he seems to have tired of authorship and in 1746 all the material was handed to Benjamin Robins* who completed the task under Anson's close supervision. Not until 1761 was it firmly stated that Robins was the author and in 1778 a note to that effect in Kippis's *Biographia Britannica* was not questioned by Walter who was still alive.

In my first edition there is a considerable number of notes in an almost illegible hand. From one of these on the flyleaf it is just possible to read the words: 'This work – – – published under the name of the Rev. Richard Walter the Chaplain was really written by Benjamin Robins – – –'

Walter's name, however, remained on the title page. The point does not affect the story in any way except to explain the change from first to third person after *Centurion*'s arrival at Macao when Walter decided to leave the expedition and return home.

The story is not nowadays widely known, the exciting events of our own time having eclipsed those of two to four centuries ago which were, however, of equally great impact on their day and age. As Walter's ponderous style of writing is unlikely to appeal to a modern reader, I have freely adapted his text and dropped most of the sermonising in which he indulged.

---

* Benjamin Robins (1707–1751) was a Fellow of the Royal Society and Engineer-General to the Honourable East India Company. James Wilson, who published Robins's mathematical and other treatises in two volumes after his death, claimed that his author was also responsible for the major part of the account of Anson's voyage.

In his introduction Walter lets himself go in urging his readers to a more considered appreciation of geography and nautical and mechanical engineering. He was very much concerned at the great interest in the naval sciences being taken by our Continental neighbours and he quotes the instance of a Mr. Frezier being sent by Louis XIV in 1711 to the South Seas. Mr. Frezier's job was to chart the coasts and the fortifications on them which, in case of a rupture with Spain, might be attacked with readiness and assurance: and Walter argues for the French example to be followed by the English.

According to him we were short of 'engineers' skilled at the drawing of such features. He proceeds at some length to discuss the importance of drawing and, although in his dedication he sounds a pompous old cleric, my heart warms to him in his insistence on drawing as a skill to be acquired by all travellers. The gentlemen of the Navy, he says, must of necessity have this ability otherwise they can make no charts or views and without them navigation must come to a full stop. Hence His Majesty had established a drawing master in the Royal (Naval) Academy at Portsmouth for the benefit of those who were later to be in positions of command.

It appears, however, that there were a number of people who considered such accomplishments effeminate and derogatory to the character of men-o'-war, but Walter then points to the drawings done by Lieutenant Brett for his book and, as he was an officer who had distinguished himself both martially and artistically and was 'at home with the Geometry, Geography and Astronomy' which were so essential to the navigation of the ship, the author considers his point clinched.

There can be no doubt of the good sense in these ideas. Mariners of the time relied strongly on the pictorial evidence of others who had previously visited strange places: and the man who could make such records was of considerable value to an expedition. Brett was no doubt such a one—excellent at charts and views, although his drawings now strike us as quaint. They were not intended, of course, to be illustrations in the modern sense. I know of no illustrated edition of Anson's voyage showing the seamen at their work and this is a lack I have thought it worth while in this case to rectify. So much of the human side, which was commonplace at that time, when seen through our eyes presents a picture of suffering and endurance of no mean order. Those of Anson's original force who managed to return after nearly four years spent in sailing round the world were lucky indeed and every man in it, officers included, must have had his health seriously impaired by the hardships he had endured.

Of the men themselves little is known, as very few would have the ability, time or desire to write their experiences. So much has to be surmised that some knowledge of what life on board ship was like and of the conditions of the service is necessary for a full appreciation of Anson's magnificent accomplishment.

He gave a victory to Britain that the country applauded handsomely.  He was rewarded in due course and afterwards became First Lord of the Admiralty in which capacity he did excellent work for the Navy's administration, although nowadays his labours seem to have been forgotten.

His splendid adventure was probably eclipsed by the achievements of Nelson at the end of the century, but to leave him in this semiobscurity is hardly fair either to him or ourselves.  The examples of the lives of such men as Anson are too valuable to be lost to any generation.

# Biographical Note

GEORGE ANSON was the second son of William Anson of Shugborough, Staffordshire. His great-grandfather was an eminent barrister in the reign of James I who built the family mansion where George was born in 1697. His mother was the daughter of Charles Carrier of Wirksworth in Derbyshire. His uncle, Thomas Parker, became Lord Chancellor in 1718 and three years later was created Earl of Macclesfield: and it is probable that Anson owed his early promotion in the Navy to this family connection. Little is known of his early life and one can only conjecture as to how he entered the service—although he was perhaps nominated as a Captain's Letter Boy by some friend of his father's, but the first certainty is that in 1712 he was a 'volunteer into the *Ruby*', in which he served for six weeks, most of them at the Nore. In the same year he joined the *Monmouth* in which he went to Jamaica.

In 1716 he was acting Lieutenant in the *Hampshire*, a rapid advance which must have been consequent upon his abilities rather than his family connections. His rank was soon confirmed and in 1718 he was in the *Montague* as 2nd Lieutenant taking part in the battle of Passaro under Sir George Byng. In 1719 he was in the *Barfleur* in which he served for two years during which he was made commander and given the *Weazle*, at that time employed on fishery protection in the North Sea. He became Captain of the frigate *Scarborough* in 1724 at the age of twenty-six and was sent to South Carolina to attack pirates and put down illicit trading in the Bahamas. His popularity in that area is reflected in the number of place-names of which Anson forms part. He was on this duty for six years after which he transferred from the *Scarborough* to the *Garland*—a similar frigate—in 1728. Returning from America he took command of the *Squirrel* from which he was quickly moved into the *Diamond* in which he served in the Mediterranean under Sir Charles Wager. Once more, this time in the *Squirrel,* he went pirate hunting in South Carolina returning in 1735 to Spithead where he paid off his ship. He remained without a command for two-and-a-half years.

During his nine years of service on the Carolina coast he became a great social favourite in the community. Diaries written at the time disclose that he was no mean performer with the cards and likewise that he was well accomplished with the bottle. The profits from his gaming he soon began to invest in real estate, his first purchase being 64 acres of plantation lands, made on 23rd March, 1726. In 1730 he returned to England leaving an agent to manage his property during his absence. On 29th September of that year there exists the record of a purchase 'to George Anson of the Middle Temple, London, late commander of H.M.S. *Garland,* a certain barony or tract of land in South Carolina comprising 12,000 acres of land'.

In 1732 he returned to Charleston in the *Squirrel.* He was soon winning large sums at cards and these were promptly put to the purchase of more land. In 1735 he bought a property in the city and 350 acres of land in Berkeley County. Further acquisitions were made around the town after which he left for England and never again returned to Carolina.

It is thus apparent that Anson could have been under no financial embarrassment when he set out on his famous voyage. A great deal of expense fell upon the commander of such an expedition— the ships were issued with the regulation allowances only and the captain and officers provided any extras which they might deem necessary. The entertainment of important visitors, the food and

*Shugborough*

*Lady Anson*

drink they would consume and the presents which in the commander's view it would be politic to make to them, were at his charge. His dress coat with its gold lace, his sword and buckles; the ceremonial dresses for his barge's crew; any personal servants above the allowed number, all these were the responsibility of the commander and the cost of them had to come from his pocket. Freedom from such worries must have been of considerable help to Anson.

On 9th December, 1737, Anson was appointed to the *Centurion*, an association which was to become as famous as Nelson with the *Victory*, or Drake with the *Golden Hind*. This commission was no doubt very welcome to the Captain after his period of unemployment and his spirits undoubtedly rose when he went off to the African coast. His duties were to harass French men-o'-war and to protect our merchantmen in the gum trade. In the autumn of 1739 he was sent to Barbados, but war having been declared he was recalled and during the next four years was engaged in the expedition which is recounted in Walter's book. When he returned in June, 1744, the bearer of his own good tidings, it was to a delighted country anxious to applaud him. He became M.P. for Hedon in Yorkshire, but he was no politician. Although politics did not interest him he became a victim of political intrigue and, thus enmeshed, he committed one or two mistaken acts which tarnished his otherwise spotless image. No appointments were ever made by him for political reasons. In 1747 after his splendid victory over the French at Finisterre, where he destroyed every one of the warships under Admiral Jonquièrre, he was raised to the peerage with the title of Baron Anson of Soberton. Four years later he was made First Lord of the Admiralty.

In 1748 he married Elizabeth, daughter of Lord Chancellor Hardwicke. This was a happy union which terminated on the death of Lady Anson in 1760. There were no children.

In 1758 he commanded the fleet before Brest covering the British landings and re-embarked the troops into his ships after their repulse.

In 1761 he sailed from Harwich in the *Charlotte* yacht to convey the future Queen of George III to England and in 1762 whilst assisting at the ceremony of accompanying the Queen's brother, Prince George of Mecklenburg, to Portsmouth, he caught a severe cold which proved fatal on 6th June, 1762. -1697 = 65

Anson was an unassuming man, slow to decide but quick to execute. He was modest, reserved, and in correspondence or matters of ceremony, he was awkward. He was obviously a man's man and his strength of character is clearly shown in his handling of his commission in the years 1740–44. Of his sixty-five years at least fifty— probably more—were spent in the Navy or at the Admiralty so that he had very little time for indulgence in the arts or cultural activities, except music which he loved. He was fifty-one when he married and although he had no real enemies, some people disliked him— Walpole for one—but no one could question his honesty or integrity.

His share of the spoils taken from the Spaniards on his great voyage made him a rich man: and it is good to find that one who had done so much for his country was able to enjoy some comfort in his life. It hasn't always happened that way.

*Some of the healthiest
walked out*

# PART ONE

# South Seas
# Project

# 1

# The Commission

IN OCTOBER, 1739, war was declared between Great Britain and Spain. As recently as January Walpole's government had signed a convention in Madrid which was intended to settle the differences between the two countries, but mounting popular clamour at home forced the administration's hand. After thirty years of peace the country frankly wanted war. Influential commercial interests in London, Bristol and other centres were determined to obtain a share in the lucrative trade with the Spanish colonies in central and southern America and proposed to achieve this by force. Other factors, which are outside the scope of this narrative, also played their part in building up the public demand for action against Spain, but commercial gain was the principal one and it inspired schemes for a series of naval expeditions against Spanish overseas possessions, including the one that was to make Anson famous.

When war broke out, Anson was at Barbados commanding the *Centurion*. He was recalled and reached Spithead on 10th November. In London he found that three separate projects were being considered by Sir Charles Wager, the First Lord of the Admiralty, and Admiral of the Fleet Sir John Norris. Admiral Vernon had already sailed with a fleet for the Caribbean where he was to harry enemy shipping and attack strongpoints on the mainland if and when an opportunity occurred. In addition to this expedition, which was the main British thrust at the start of hostilities, Wager was considering two smaller ventures which had the same purpose, the destruction of Spanish trade and possessions overseas. The first of these, suggested by Hubert Tassell and Henry Hutchinson, two former agents of the South Sea Company, was a plan to send 1,500 soldiers round Cape Horn to assault the settlements on the Pacific coast. The second scheme, proposed by James Naish, a one-time supercargo in the East India Company, was to capture Manilla in the Philippines, the base from which the great treasure galleons made their annual voyage across the Pacific. It was the second of these expeditions, the assault on Manilla, that Anson was chosen to command.

As at this time planned, Anson's squadron was to take on board three independent companies of a hundred men each and Bland's Regiment of Foot. The Colonel of this regiment was to command the land forces. The squadron was to commence fitting out at once and when under way to touch at no place till they arrived at Java Head in the East Indies. After taking in water there, they were to proceed to Manilla in the Philippines.

The other squadron, of the same strength as Anson's, was intended to go round the Horn and inflict as much damage as possible on the enemy on the Pacific coasts after which they were to rendezvous with Anson at Manilla. The combined squadrons were to rest and refit there and wait for further orders.

The scheme was an ambitious one but it had Sir Charles Wager's whole-hearted support.

On 18th November Anson received orders to take under his command the *Argyle, Severn, Pearl, Wager*, and *Tryal* sloop. Preparations for fitting out and victualling were well in hand, when early in January, 1740, Anson was told that the Manilla project was cancelled. Instead his squadron was to undertake the South Sea expedition round the Horn. Its composition remained unchanged except that the *Gloucester* was substituted for the *Argyle*. On 10th January he received his commission as Commander-in-Chief. Anson pressed on with the equipping of his ships, hoping to make an early start. By this time Portsmouth had become a very busy place. Ships were fitting out for their long journeys to the Caribbean and the Pacific. Men-o'-war and transports destined for the West Indies were loading arms and equipment and all the supplies necessary to stage a campaign there. For the Pacific venture great quantities of foodstuffs and stores were being prepared—more, declared Anson, than any fleet had ever before carried. The dockyard workshops were humming with the activities of the craftsmen busy at their carpentry, rope spinning, coopering and baking; the armourers and sailmakers, the blacksmiths and tinsmiths were all turning out their products as fast as they could go. And it is not hard to imagine the work being done by needlewomen and tailors in all sorts of small establishments on the shirts and underwear and the jackets and trousers for the thousands of soldiers and sailors who were shortly setting off. No sewing machines in those days.

On 28th June, 1740, the Duke of Newcastle gave Anson His Majesty's instructions, with some additions from the Lords Justices.*

* In 1740 the 'Lords Justices' were persons appointed by the Sovereign to act for a time as his substitute in the supreme Government during the King's absence in his German territories.

The first instructions, signed by the King, were dated 31st January, the additional instructions 19th June (Appendix I and II). By them Anson's primary objective was defined as being to 'annoy the Spaniards', in other words the destruction of Spanish shipping and trade along the Pacific coast. The instructions also envisaged attacks on Callao, where the colonists were thought to be ready to rebel against the Spanish Crown, on Panama and even on points across the isthmus where Anson could join forces with Vernon's forces: and for these land operations Anson was to embark 500 troops. Finally, the possibility of capturing the Manilla treasure galleon was mentioned. In all this Anson was given considerable discretion. One point is of especial interest, as significant of Anson's determination. The instructions foresaw that the squadron might reach Cape Horn at the worst time of year and therefore authorised Anson to winter in the River Plate. In fact he did arrive at the Horn when conditions were at their worst but he chose to press on, ignoring this special authority to take shelter until they improved.

By June the fitting out of the squadron was well advanced and Anson's main concern was to find the troops promised in his orders and the crews for his six ships. An application to Sir John Norris who commanded at Spithead was abruptly turned down, as the admiral was short of men himself. Further delay followed. Sir John Balchen shortly replaced Norris but he was only able to provide 170 men—32 from the hospital and sick quarters, 37 from the *Salisbury* and 3 officers of Colonel Lowther's regiment with 98 marines. These last were commanded by Lieutenant-Colonel Mordaunt Cracherode. To make good his deficiency Anson was told to receive—and it is easy to imagine his feelings—500 Invalids from Chelsea Hospital. The employment of these men, many enfeebled by age or maimed by wounds, seems barely credible, but, in spite of protests from Sir Charles Wager, the military authorities decided that they would be perfectly adequate for a protracted voyage in which extreme hardships were certain to be met. In the event only 259 came aboard, many over sixty years old and some over seventy.

In order to understand fully the use of Invalids, we have to go back to 1688 when there was a threat of invasion. It was necessary to have regular troops ready for field work and in order to relieve them from garrison duties, companies of Invalids were formed from the pensioners at Chelsea Hospital.

A typical company at this time consisted of 1 captain, 2 lieutenants, 1 ensign, 6 sergeants, 6 corporals, 2 drummers and 150 men. Their uniform and equipment consisted of a hat, coat and breeches, neckcloth, shoes and stockings and shirts and a sword-belt and arms. The dress was the same as the Royal Hospital uniform with single-breasted red coat with blue facings and blue breeches. The coat had the Royal Cipher at front and back.

In 1719 the Regiment of Invalids was formed and numbered the 41st of the line. Inspection returns give the picture of the type of man filling the ranks of the Invalids.

> The Officers are old and mostly wounded and infirm. Many have lost limbs, many of the men are stout. One major was 82 years old and other officers not much younger. Two were stone blind and the average age was 50 to 60.

When drafts were needed for the Invalid companies a number of out-patients were ordered to Chelsea by notices in the press. Failure to report incurred the loss of pension.

The reason for calling up these old-timers for service with Anson is understandable in view of the military situation. The main effort against the Spanish colonies was to be made in the Caribbean and the best men were wanted for that enterprise. Anson's task was to harry the Spanish shipping and to do as many 'annoyances' as possible. It was not expected that large-scale land operations would be necessary on the Pacific coast.

Nevertheless, Anson lost a number of the more able-bodied of his 259 invalids before his voyage started. Some of the healthiest of the sorry band, when they learned of the expedition's destination, as rumoured on the lower deck, walked out of Portsmouth as fast as they could go, pension or no pension, leaving their less able comrades to serve King and country. From the outset, therefore, the squadron was handicapped by the inclusion of cripples and the infirm. No special provision could be made for these men who were expected to share the same conditions as their shipmates—poor rations and only fifteen inches in which to swing their hammocks. The so-called hospital facilities, vividly described by Tobias Smollett who served as a surgeon's mate in 1741, were reserved for serious cases, and Anson, a humane commander, could do nothing to improve their lot. It is not surprising that not one of them survived the rigours of the voyage.

As if his anxieties were not already enough, Anson was obliged to accept against his better judgment the service of two agent victuallers who had been in the employment of the South Sea Company. Their previous experience, it was believed, had made them expert in bartering for food and other supplies from the natives. For this purpose they were to take on board some £15,000 of merchandise, which was, according to them, of more use than money in trading. The Commodore, says Walter, objected from the beginning, both to the appointment of the agents and the carriage of the goods, for he was certain that in most places he could persuade the natives to let him have what he wanted without the aid of agents. It was his opinion also that £2,000 or £3,000 worth of stuff might be sufficient to tempt the Indians or Spanish planters in the less frequented parts of the coast for he was also certain that these were the only people who would be prepared to do business. Another point of view was expressed by Sir John Norris who thought it was not right for His Majesty's ships to carry goods as such action would suggest that the vessels were being used for a private trade. However, the Government agreed to lend £10,000 towards the scheme and the remaining £5,000 was raised on bottomry bonds.*

Shortly before the squadron sailed a final reinforcement reached Anson consisting of 210 marines drawn from different regiments. These men were all new recruits, completely untrained, who at the time of their embarkation had not yet been allowed to fire their muskets. Their arrival marked the end of Anson's tribulations on shore and on 10th August he sailed with his squadron to St. Helens in the Isle of Wight to wait for a favouring wind.

The Squadron at its outset consisted of the following ships:

| | |
|---|---|
| The *Centurion* | of sixty guns with 400 men with George Anson as Captain and Commodore of the Squadron. |
| The *Gloucester* | (Richard Norris) and |
| The *Severn* | (Hon. Edward Legge), both of fifty guns and 300 men. |
| The *Pearl* | (Mathew Mitchell) with forty guns and 250 men. |
| The *Wager* | (Dandy Kidd) with twenty-eight guns and 160 men. |
| The *Tryal* Sloop | (Hon. George Murray) with eight guns and 100 men. |
| *Industry* | Victualler—400 tons. |
| *Anna* Pink | Victualler—200 tons. |

It was now very late in the year to start the voyage. In addition Anson was ordered to sail in company with a fleet under the command of Admiral Balchen. There were in this combined fleet twenty-one warships and 124 merchantmen and transports. A mass of vessels like this would need good constant winds to enable them to get clear of the Channel and at that time of the year such a condition was chancy indeed. In fact it was forty days before Anson's squadron did get away from St. Helens and even then they had orders to sail without Admiral Balchen.

* Bottomry bonds are a form of mortgage on the ship by which money to enable it to proceed on its voyage is raised. The ship with all cargo and freight is made liable for the repayment.

The fleet tried a number of times without success to make its way down Channel and during their enforced stay some of the transports were damaged in a gale and all the ships had to strike their topmasts and yards to prevent their driving.*

On 12th September Anson received orders to take under his protection the *St. Albans* and the *Lark* with a convoy, bound for the Eastern Mediterranean, and to join a similar fleet on its way to America under the charge of the *Dragon* and the *Winchester*, and to proceed with these two convoys as far as possible. At last on 18th September, Anson, now in full command, sent instructions to the America convoy at Torbay to be ready for him as soon as he arrived. This he picked up off Rame Head on the 20th and getting a favourable wind he made his way down Channel which he cleared in four days.

Such then was the start of a naval task force designed to strike a serious blow at Spanish possessions on the other side of the world. The senseless chopping and changing of plan, the disgraceful and short-sighted substitution of pensioners, invalids and raw recruits for seamen and marines, were serious hazards for Anson. The delays occasioned by the arguments and discussions of all these problems were the cause of the very late start, the result of which was to ensure that the Squadron would round the Horn in the southern winter.

The long period of waiting had allowed time for news of the expedition to reach the Spanish Government. Confirmation of this was received on 6th June when two British ships in Caribbean waters captured a Dutch vessel carrying the Viceroy of Mexico and his retinue. The Viceroy escaped in a fast sloop, but in his hurry left behind a trunk of papers. On examination these proved beyond doubt that the Spanish Government had full knowledge of Anson's fleet and its objectives: also that warnings had been sent to Peru and Mexico to put the authorities on their guard. As if to ensure full publicity, the London papers during July printed reports on the expedition and on its probable date of sailing.

---

* As Anson's Squadron had to do this many times during the voyage a word of explanation may be in order. Masts and rigging present considerable 'windage' and in heavy gales it was the practice to lower as much as possible of this 'top-hamper' to relieve the ship from the tremendous pressure above. The task of 'striking' topmasts was a regular chore on old sailing ships.

# 2

# The Squadron Sails

WHEN ANSON was finally under way with his convoys he was in command of a fleet of 11 men-o'-war and 141 merchantmen. He hoisted his broad pennant and calling his naval captains on board gave them their fighting and sailing instructions for the first leg of the voyage: and with a fair wind all the ships stood to the south-west. By 29th September the last of the convoys had separated from the Commodore, and his little Squadron kept on course alone for Madeira. The weather deteriorated and their progress was so slow that it required forty days after leaving St. Helens to reach the islands—a journey frequently completed in ten or twelve days.

For a week they stayed at Madeira, watering the ships and refreshing the men. Whilst here, Captain Norris requested permission to relinquish his command of the *Gloucester* on account of ill health and this he was allowed to do. Anson moved Captain Mitchell to the *Gloucester* and Captain Kidd from the *Wager* to the *Pearl*, and Captain Murray from the *Tryal* to the *Wager* and command of the *Tryal* sloop was given to Lieutenant Cheap.

On 4th November the captains received their instructions for the journey to the next point—St. Jago in the Cape Verde Islands. They were to rendezvous there and if they did not find the *Centurion*, to make the best of their way to St. Catherine's on the coast of Brazil. These sailing instructions were later altered to omit the call at St. Jago. All provisions being laid in, preparations were made to leave Madeira.

On 28th November they crossed the line and Millechamp, the purser of the *Tryal*,* gives the version of the ceremony performed on the initiates as practised in his day. The victim was obliged to pay his bottle and pound, the bottle being of rum or brandy and the

---

* Later in this expedition he also served in the *Gloucester* and *Centurion* as well as the *Tryal's Prize.*

9

pound, of sugar.  Refusal either from poverty or obstinacy was punished by ducking.  The man was hoisted by a tackle to the main or foreyard.  He was then let drop 'sowse over head and ears in the water.  This they repeat until the offender is as wet as a drowned rat.  They then take him in and as he has contributed so much to their mirth they suffer him to partake of their liquor till he is thoroughly drenched both inside and out.'

During his short stay at Madeira the Commodore had learnt from the Governor that at the end of October seven or eight ships and a small vessel, presumed to be French or Spanish, had appeared to the west of the island.  Anson immediately sent a fast sloop to reconnoitre, but there was no sight of any enemy, but it seemed certain that the ships were a Spanish fleet whose purpose was to put a stop to his expedition.  By the accident of the two fleets being on opposite sides of the island, no contact between them was established. The Spaniards having learnt that Anson had sailed with Balchen's fleet waited until they thought the Commodore was on his own.  This Spanish Squadron, although it never met or fought with Anson, suffered in every way very much as the English fleet, and Walter gives the history of it at some length.

The Spanish fleet comprised a considerable part of the naval power of Spain which was diverted from the European theatre and finally lost—a loss of ships and men which was the direct consequence of the enemy having to take measures against Anson.

The Spanish Squadron which was sent out for this purpose was commanded by Don José Pizarro.  It consisted of five vessels:

| The *Asia* | of 66 guns | 700 men—the Admiral |
|---|---|---|
| The *Guipuscoa* | 74 ,, | 700 ,, |
| The *Hermiona* | 54 ,, | 500 ,, |
| The *Esperanza* | 50 ,, | 450 ,, |
| The *St. Estevan* | 40 ,, | 350 ,, |

a patache of twenty guns and two other ships which parted from the main fleet after leaving Madeira.

Apart from the complement of sailors and marines Pizarro's ships carried a regiment of foot intended for the reinforcement of garrisons on the South Seas coast.

This fleet left the Madeiras in the beginning of November at approximately the same time as Anson, and arrived off the mouth of the River Plate on 8th January, 1741, where Pizarro sent to Buenos Aires immediately for provisions.  He had sailed from Spain with only four months' supplies and must by this time have been getting short of necessities.  However, on receiving the news from the

Portuguese Governor of St. Catherine's, that Anson had arrived at that place and was preparing to leave, Pizarro weighed from the Plate after only seventeen days' sojourn and without the provisions he so urgently needed for the next stage of his journey.

Anson left St. Catherine's about four days before Pizarro cleared from the Plate, and during their passage to Cape Horn the two fleets were so close that at one time the *Pearl*, being accidentally separated from the rest of Anson's Squadron, fell in with the Spanish fleet and mistaking the *Asia* for the *Centurion* narrowly missed being shot up.

Having reached the latitude of the Horn Pizarro stood westward in preparation for rounding the stormy cape but on the first night of this new course the *Guipuscoa*, the *Hermiona* and the *Esperanza* were separated from the Admiral. A week later the *Guipuscoa* lost sight of the other two. Before she had got very far a furious storm blowing from the north-west drove them back eastward and after a fearful struggle against the weather they gave up and decided to go back to the River Plate. The *Asia*, the *Esperanza* and the *St. Estevan* arrived there two months later. The *Hermiona* must have

'*Sowse over head and ears in the water*'

foundered for she was never heard of again and the *Guipuscoa* was later lost on the coast of Brazil.

Both the Spanish and English Squadrons underwent the same trials off the Horn, the same ravages of storms and damage, but whilst Anson's men were stricken with scurvy the Spanish crews faced the additional hazard of famine.   Rats were sold on the Spanish ships at four dollars apiece.   The shortage of food in due course led to attempted mutiny.   In the nick of time Pizarro discovered a conspiracy among the marines on the *Asia* to murder the officers and crew thereby obtaining the remaining food for themselves. The ringleaders of the plot were put to death, but this did not ease the general distress, and the three ships which had survived the storms continued to lose heavily from starvation.   The *Asia* and the *St. Estevan* both lost half of their complement; of 450 on the *Esperanza* only fifty-eight survived and the regiment of foot was reduced to fifty men.

The details of the fate of the *Guipuscoa* came into the hands of Anson later.   There is little question but that her crew endured much the same struggles as the English, for in that first storm, after losing the *Hermiona* and *Esperanza* in a fog, the mainsail split and they had to bear away under foresail, with the sail often under water.   The mainmast sprung and the ship was making water so fast that with four pumps and baling they could not get it under.   The gales continued for over a week: and then the sea was so high and the ship rolling so terribly that she opened up the seams and butts of her planking and top timbers, the bolts drawing in the violent motion. With practically no food and continuing disasters to hull and rigging, they at last gave up trying to make to the west and, with men dying from the labour of pumping and the severe weather, turned back towards the River Plate.   All the upper deck guns and an anchor were thrown overboard and they took six turns with a cable round the ship to prevent her opening up.   Later, in a heavy swell with no wind, she rolled the main, fore and mizen masts right out and the men had to cut away the bowsprit to ease the leak at the head.   Such was the state of the *Guipuscoa* a month after reaching the Horn!

Two hundred and fifty men had perished from hunger and fatigue and the rest were on the tiniest allowance of biscuit.   Men died at the pumps and for three weeks it was impossible to rig jury masts so that the ship drove like a wreck till it reached the coast of Brazil at Rio de Patas, ten leagues to the south of the Island of St. Catherine's. The captain, anxious to save his ship, wanted to get to St. Catherine's, but the crew ceased pumping and demanded that the ship be brought to shore where they were.   With thirty dead bodies lying on the deck the Captain could do nothing but comply and he ran the ship in to the coast. Five days later he sank the vessel with all her furniture and the remainder of her stores. Four hundred of the ship's company who had survived this shocking voyage were saved.

When Pizarro in the *Asia* arrived at the River Plate with the three remaining ships of his squadron he immediately sent an advice boat to Rio de Janeiro with a letter of credit to purchase what he could from the Portuguese. At the same time he sent a dispatch across the continent to the Viceroy of Peru telling him of the disaster to his squadron and asking for 200,000 dollars to refit and revictual the remaining ships for another attempt on the Horn in the good season. But the Viceroy sent only half the sum asked for.

There was disappointment also when the advice boat returned from Rio for although it brought back plenty of pitch, tar and cordage, no masts or spars had been acquired. Pizarro was obliged to take the masts of the *Esperanza* and adapt them for the *Asia* and by using all spare spars in the three ships he refitted the *Asia* and the *St. Estevan*. By October, 1741, Pizarro was ready to make his second attempt on Cape Horn, but ill-luck still dogged him. The *St. Estevan* managed to leave her rudder on a shoal and suffered such extensive damage that the Admiral had her broken up. Valiantly he set out once more in the only ship left to him. Off the Horn the *Asia* was again dismasted and again put back to the Plate. The *Esperanza* which had been left behind without her masts was

*The ships had to strike their topmasts*

now refitted and in November the following year she sailed and, having made a good passage, arrived safely on the coast of Chile where Pizarro, who had crossed overland, met her. During her voyage she had been commanded by Mindinetta who now challenged Pizarro's right to command on the ground that he had forfeited it by taking the overland route. The dispute was protracted and only settled after an appeal to higher authority—in Pizarro's favour.

The *Esperanza* was finally left in the South Seas while Mindinetta and Pizarro returned overland to Buenos Aires in 1745 to find the *Asia* at Montevideo. They decided to take this ship back to Europe, refitting her for the journey as best they could. But the greatest difficulty lay in manning her for there were not a hundred sailors to be found in all the neighbourhood of Buenos Aires. They set sail about November, 1745, and very soon had a near-successful rebellion on their hands. This was engineered by eleven Indians who had been impressed into the crew with English and Portuguese prisoners and a good number of citizens of Buenos Aires. These eleven Indians, led by one Orellana, succeeded in mastering the ship for two hours before Orellana was shot dead, upon which his companions jumped into the sea. Escaping from this last danger Pizarro arrived on the coast of Galicia in the beginning of 1746.

This expedition had cost the Spanish navy over 3,000 men and four great ships of war. The *Asia* with a hundred hands was all that remained of the squadron which Pizarro had taken out to destroy Anson.

Pearl *fell in with the Spanish fleet*

# 3

# South to Cape Horn

THE SEASON was getting late when Anson left Madeira. Accordingly he decided that it would be better to push on directly to St. Catherine's without touching at St. Jago in the Cape Verde Islands, as required by the Admiralty orders, and he issued instructions to this effect to the fleet.

On 16th November, 1740, the master of the *Industry*, one of the victualling ships, asked to be unloaded and dismissed. The victuallers were on charter and were at liberty to return home when their job had been completed. On investigation all the ships were found to be so laden with provisions that it was going to be difficult to squeeze anything more into them, but they were ordered to heave to and take their shares of the brandy in the *Industry* pink. The long boats of the squadron needed three days for this work, and, when it was completed, the *Industry* left the Squadron and sailed for Barbados. This ship was later captured by the Spaniards.

By 10th December, the Squadron was in soundings off the coast of Brazil. During the journey from Madeira many men had died from sickness and as many were confined to their hammocks, several of them being past hope of recovery. Tropical fevers and scurvy were beginning to take a serious toll of the crews so that it must have been with relief that they sighted the island of St. Catherine's off the coast of Brazil on 18th December. They came to anchor and were made rudely aware that their presence had alarmed the coast. Two forts immediately fired several guns. In spite of this demonstration, Anson sent a boat on shore to compliment the Governor and to request a pilot to take him into the port.

Earlier voyagers had reported this place as being healthy and well provided which gave the Squadron hopes of curing their sick and replenishing their stores of fresh food. As soon as the ships were moored the sick men were carried ashore, each ship erecting two tents for their accommodation. The *Centurion* alone sent eighty men, or a fifth of her whole company, and the other ships in much the same proportion. Anson gave orders for the ships to be cleansed throughout, by fumigation and washing with vinegar! The vessels stank abominably; they were alive with vermin, and sickness and the heat had made them offensive even to men hardened in the service. It was generally believed that these insanitary conditions were a cause of their bad bill of health.

While this work was in progress, preparations for the next stage of the voyage were put in hand: watering, wooding, caulking sides and decks, repairing rigging and getting fresh shrouds and stays to the masts in readiness for the violent weather that would most likely assault them on their passage round the Horn. Anson did his best to ensure that all hands should be supplied with fresh meat, vegetables and fruit during their stay at St. Catherine's, but with only mediocre results. Pascoe Thomas, the schoolmaster in the *Centurion*, described their state at this time:

> The agents for victualling, of which we had two with us, were ordered to procure what fresh provisions we could expend during our stay here, which they accordingly did; but though their meat, which was all-together beef, was both cheap and plenty, it was for the greatest part miserably bad, and scarce fit to be eaten. The men throughout the whole squadron began now to drop off apace with fevers and fluxes, occasioned, I believe, by the violent heat of the climate, and the bad air; the country being so very woody that the air must thereby be stagnated, and rendered unhealthful.

There was no incentive to delay further at St. Catherine's and Anson was extremely anxious to sail before the weather should deteriorate, but to his dismay it was reported that the *Tryal*'s masts were in a bad way—the mainmast sprung* and the fore was rotten. Her captain hoped that the mainmast could be fished. Fishing was the lashing of strong timbers alongside the weak place to give it support. The foremast was useless and carpenters were sent ashore to find a tree that would provide a reasonable spar, but four days' search produced nothing. So they had to fish both masts and while they were at it they had the *Tryal* hove down for cleaning her bottom.

---

* A 'spring' in a mast was a crack occurring transversely across the shaft. The depth of the break could be assessed from the length of the visible line around the circumference of the mast. The drying out of the timber and violent strains on the rigging during gales were the causes of springs.

Six days after their arrival a Portuguese brigantine arrived in the anchorage. Anson sent his eighteen-oared barge to determine whether the vessel was Spanish, but to his surprise the Portuguese Governor took great pains to prevent his men from getting aboard this craft. At the time the reason for this action was not clear. In fact, the Governor had already secretly reported the arrival of the English squadron to Pizarro who was at Buenos Aires, giving a detailed account of its strength and condition, and he had a lively fear that Anson might hear of his treachery if his officers made contact with those of the brigantine. It was only many months later that Anson discovered the truth of the matter.

Four weeks were required to complete repairs and in that time as much refitting and renovating as possible was carried out in every ship of the Squadron. Bearing in mind the tempestuous weather which he could expect around the Horn, Anson had the ships send some of their larger guns down into the holds, which would allow them to carry more sail and make an easier passage. At last the fleet was ready. The tents ashore were struck and the sick men returned aboard. St. Catherine's, for all its reputation, had not improved the health of the crews. Although the *Centurion* had sent eighty sick men ashore and had buried twenty-eight men since her arrival, no fewer than ninety-six sick men were re-embarked when the time came to put to sea. Millechamp summed up the general opinion: 'In short all I can say of this island is that it is a glorious garden in the hands of a bad manager.'

Anson called his captains and issued orders for the successive places of rendezvous all the way to Chile, and the Squadron left St. Catherine's on 18th January, 1741, with no regrets.

Anson framed his instructions with particular care. From now on the Squadron could expect nothing but opposition from the elements with little prospect of shelter on the hostile and inhospitable coasts. In Cape Horn weather the sudden separation of the ships was only too likely and this was a danger to be avoided at all costs.

*Tents ashore*

Accordingly he appointed a number of stations on his route at which the ships were to rendezvous and prescribed the action to be taken in the event of the loss of the *Centurion*. The expedition was to go forward no matter what happened.

The first place of call was to be St. Julian, where they were to take in as much salt as possible. If the Commodore had not turned up in ten days from their arrival the other ships were to go through the Straits of Lemaire round the Horn into the South Sea. The next rendezvous was to be the island of Nostra Señora del Socorro, to the west of the Chonos Archipelago off the coast of Chile. They were to cruise up and down from 30 to 60 miles to the ENE for as long as their fuel and water lasted and when it became essential to procure more they were to go in and find a place to land. In case of bad weather they were to proceed as best they could to Juan Fernandez, in latitude 33°50 S. If after replenishing and after fifty-six days of cruising in the vicinity of the island, there was still no sign of the

*A spring in the mainmast*

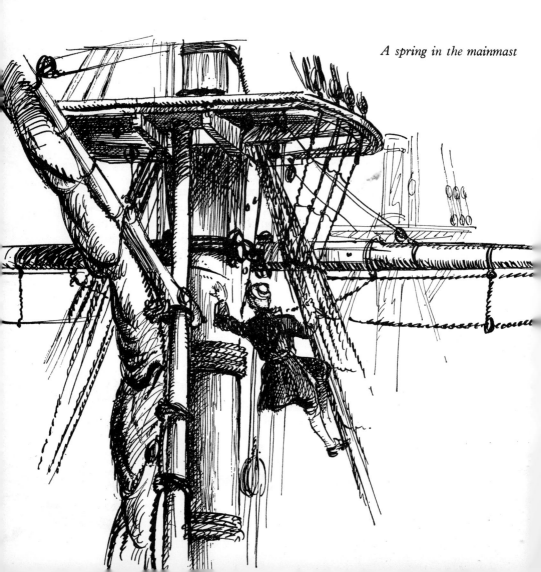

Commodore the senior officer present was to assume command of the Squadron and proceed with the original plan to harass the enemy in the Pacific. The remaining victualling vessel—the *Anna* pink— was put under the same orders.

They sailed on a Sunday. On the Thursday following the fleet was struck by a violent storm accompanied by a thick fog in which the ships lost sight of each other. For four hours this fog persisted and when it cleared the *Pearl* was nowhere to be seen. The *Tryal* had lost her mainmast and the *Gloucester* took her in tow. During the gale *Tryal* was compelled to take two reefs in each topsail and a sudden gust carried away the head of the mainmast and all the spars and rigging above it went overboard. Eight men who were on the main topsail yard went with it and all but one were fortunately saved. This last man was tangled in the fallen rigging and drowned when it was cut away. Millechamp wrote: 'The seven men they saved were all cut and bruised in a most terrible manner, and so as to be of no use to them for a great while.'

Nearly a month later the *Pearl* was discovered and it was learned that Captain Dandy Kidd had died. Mr. Salt, the Lieutenant in Command, reported how during his absence from the Squadron he had met five ships, the chief of which had a broad red pennant at the main topmast head which was an exact copy of Anson's. In fact this was the Spanish fleet.

Mistaking them for the rest of the squadron, Lieutenant Salt was hoisting out his boat to go on board the *Centurion* and pay his respects to the Commodore. It was only when it was noticed that the Commodore had not slung his pendant in his usual fashion that they realised the truth of the situation and hoisting all sail they escaped. Millechamp was very surprised that Don Pizarro had allowed about the worst sailer in the English Squadron to get away from five Spanish men-o'-war without a single shot being fired at her.

This news of a Spanish fleet in the vicinity was disconcerting and had it not been for the state of the *Tryal* Anson would have left St. Julian immediately. However, the sloop could not be sailed round the Horn with her damaged masts. Repairs had to be undertaken. He sent two cutters to examine the coast for a harbour and as soon as some shelter was found the carpenters got busy at the refitting of the sloop. The mainmast had fractured about 12 feet below the cap but the stump remained and on this they improvised a topmast made from a spar taken from the *Wager*. Perhaps it was as well that the *Tryal* suffered this trouble at this juncture for had she gone further the weather that later beset them would have undoubtedly destroyed her.

At St. Julian Anson wished to re-provision his ships from the *Anna* pink, but all the masters made it clear that they could take nothing more aboard.   The entire space between the guns was already crammed with great quantities of foodstuffs and the ships sat so deep in the water that should they meet with the Spanish squadron it would be impossible to fire a shot.   The Commodore decided therefore to keep the *Anna* and, far from taking provisions from her, the excess from between the ships' guns was transferred back into her in readiness for an encounter with the Spanish ships which, he felt, might occur at any time.

Here also Anson put the final touches to his preparations for rounding the Horn, an antagonist likely to prove as formidable as the warships of Spain.   Thomas records of St. Julian: 'Here we further secured our lower deck guns, by nailing quoins under the trucks, in case the tackles, breechings, or iron-work, might give way, or fail in the stormy weather which we had much reason to expect.'

Whilst waiting for the completion of the repairs to the *Tryal*, the Englishmen took note of the inhabitants' way of life, being deeply impressed by their fine horsemanship.   The cowboys hunted cattle with a lash, not a lasso, which they used with great skill.   The beasts were killed for the hides and tallow; the carcass was left to rot or given to the dogs, which, originally introduced by the Spaniards, roamed the countryside in their thousands.   They found also that horses, likewise introduced by the Spaniards, had become so numer-

*Tryal loses her mainmast*

ous and had so little value that the very best of them were sold for a dollar. The one thing the country lacked, from the seaman's point of view, was timber of which the landscape was bare. Sir John Narborough, who wintered in the neighbourhood of St. Julian in 1670, said he never saw a stick of wood in the entire area large enough to make the handle of a hatchet. The salt which Anson had instructed them to load was not to be had and it was presumed that wet weather over a long period had ruined the deposits.

The Commodore called a council of war on board the *Centurion* at which the ships' captains and Colonel Cracherode, commanding the troops, were briefed on the plan of operations. Anson's orders directed him, if at all possible, to secure a port where the ships might be careened and refitted, and he proposed that, on their arrival in the Pacific, they should attack the town of Baldivia. This is now called Valdivia and lies on the west coast of Chile in 45°S. In consequence, his instructions to the Squadron to cruise for fifty-six days off Nostra Señora del Socorro were amended to ten days at the end of which, if the *Centurion* had not appeared, the ships were to continue and cruise off the harbour of Baldivia taking care to keep well to the southward of that port. If in another fourteen days the Squadron was still incomplete they were ordered to make for Juan Fernandez. The *Anna* pink received similar orders. Separation was the danger most feared by Anson, and he made it clear that any neglect by an officer that led to separation would be severely punished.

Gloucester *takes*
Tryal *in tow*

The Squadron weighed on 27th February, 1741, when at last the *Tryal* was ready to put to sea.   The *Gloucester* got away to a slow start.   In order to keep in sight of the Squadron her crew were obliged to cut their cable and leave their best bower anchor behind. This was serious, not only in point of the loss but because the lack of the second largest anchor meant that the ship could find herself in great danger.   Accidents such as this were precisely those that might bring about the very separation Anson was so anxious to avoid.   He was so certain of meeting the Spanish squadron that he considered it imperative to keep his fleet together; and he had issued instructions for this to his captains.   With no enemies in the area he could have relaxed his control and allowed each ship to proceed as best it could.

The 4th of March, 1741, found them close to the eastern entrance to the Straits of Magellan and, the weather being bright and calm, the captains paid the Commodore a social visit.   The gathering was rudely interrupted when a burst of flame and a cloud of smoke shot up from the *Gloucester*.   Fortunately, the alarm was quickly over and the fire was soon extinguished without damage to the ship.

They began to learn the lesson that the fair weather in these latitudes is of very short duration and invariably followed by a storm.   This was exactly what now happened and the Squadron was forced to bring-to under reefed mizens.   After a day of this the wind eased and towards midnight they made sail again.   The next morning found them off the coast of Tierra del Fuego where they were impressed by the tremendous height of the snow-covered mountains.   That night the Squadron once again lay-to as they could

*Fishing a mast*

not risk over-shooting the entrance to the Straits: the watch on deck spent most of the time in bending an entirely new suit of sails.   With sailing ships that was the way of things—in good weather any old sails: in very bad conditions they had to be of the strongest canvas and as new as possible.

In the morning, 7th March, they moved to go into the Straits but found great difficulty in picking out the actual entrance owing to lack of accurate charts or pictures—a practical vindication of Walter's contention that every officer should know how to make good drawings of such places for the benefit of the mariners who should come after them.

Staten Land looked the most horrible place imaginable.   Savage and desolate, it overawed Millechamp who described it in vivid terms.   'It seems to be the vast ruins of some prodigious edifice, and is a proper nursery for desperation.'   In comparison with which Tierra del Fuego, on the other side of the Straits, seemed a perfect paradise.

In very good weather with a bright sky and the *Pearl* and *Tryal* leading, they passed through the Straits of Lemaire in about a couple of hours.   This 20-mile channel was reckoned to be the gateway from the Atlantic to the Pacific and the elation of the crews at having come through it so easily can be imagined.   They were now well on their way to relieve the Spaniards of some of the gold and silver with which they conceived their enemies to be overburdened. Walter, with the cleric's sense of the dramatic, ends his chapter with the paragraph:

Thus animated by these delusions, we travers'd these memorable streights, ignorant of the dreadful calamities that were then impending and just ready to break upon us; ignorant that the time drew near, when the Squadron would be separated never to unite again, and that this day of our passage was the last cheerful day that the greatest part of us would ever live to enjoy.

*The watch on deck
spent most of their time
bending an entirely new
suit of sails*

Mountainous seas struck
at them

# PART TWO

# Fight for
# Survival

# 4

# The Struggle Begins

THERE IS NO doubt, even allowing for Walter's style, that the odds suddenly turned against the expedition. The troubles that now beset them were those of the dreaded Cape Horn and—let there be no mistake about it—to round this Cape in a sailing vessel in severe weather was as dire an experience to which any man could be subjected who was not under-going punishment for a heinous crime.

Violent squalls known as Cape Horn Snorters develop suddenly. Great waves of over 60 feet in height covered with streaks of foam roll majestically across the ocean and the wind moans and screams without ceasing. A wave bigger than the rest with smaller seas raging on its flanks, rears its head vertically in bright translucent green and breaks along its entire ridge into 20 feet of boiling thrashing surf. Heaven help the ship which is overwhelmed by such a breaker for everything on deck will be smashed and splintered, with ironwork twisted like wire and men crushed.

But the violence is not confined to the storms. The calms that follow them are dreaded as much as the winds. The sea is still heaving tempestuously but without wind the ship cannot sail and is left rolling fearfully, down in huge troughs between and up and over the horribly steep and broken waves. A capsize was a constant hazard in such conditions while a common and dangerous consequence of this extreme rolling was for the ironwork of the rigging and the masts themselves to collapse under the strain.

28

There are numbers of stories of tough passages made during the last days of sail when science had brought about major improvements in ship design. There were plenty of officers who had made the voyage ten, twenty and even thirty times. Yet the most hard-bitten confessed to a nervous thrill whenever he crossed 50°S. Few ships escaped without some scars to show and the Horn was reckoned the fiercest enemy that seamen could expect to meet.

Anson's ships were not designed for seas such as they had to meet. In his time a ship was a ship. Some were better than others but all were meant to sail anywhere whatever the weather conditions and England was never short of men ready to match their skill against the elements, however ill-found or unsuited their ship might be for the specific task. Anson was probably ignorant of the magnitude of the seas and strength of the winds that he would encounter in the worst conditions, but, if he had known, it would have made no difference.

*Cape Horn*

Although no scale of wind velocities was in existence at this time the strength of these gales and squalls has since been measured. 60 m.p.h. winds are continuously roaring for very long periods and gusts of much greater strength are common.  His ships were in reasonable condition and his attention to hull and rigging as he came closer to the area of storms was all that, as a prudent commander, he could give.  It would never have occurred to him that with his ships so low in the water and in what might be termed second-hand condition, he was really undertaking a suicidal voyage.

However, they were not left long in doubt of the truth of the matter.  The pleasant trip through the Straits terminated with a rapidly darkening sky and a sudden change of wind.  The tide which had helped them through swung against them and a series of squalls smacked them down under reefed mainsails only.  The current pushed them rapidly eastward: and there was considerable anxiety for the safety of *Wager* and the *Anna* pink who, being astern of the Squadron, were much closer to Staten Island from which they both had the greatest difficulty in getting clear.  What with this tide and the storms, by next morning they were about 21 miles east of Staten Island.  The strength of both the current and the westerly winds not only gave them a new respect for Cape Horn but they now even began to doubt their ability to double it.

For the storm did not cease and there followed a continuous run of such tempests that the oldest and most experienced mariners had never seen the like.  Compared with what they were now experiencing they decided that what they had previously called storms were but strong breezes.  And under the pressure of these winds the seas were so short and so steep that there were none like them to be found anywhere else in the world.  They knew that if one such sea were to break over them they would be sent to the bottom.  Nor was this all, for the rolling and violent motion to which the ships were subject was killing and maiming men, who were wrenched from their hold by the strength of some of the shocks.  One of their best men on the *Centurion* was pitched overboard and drowned, one thrown down the hold, breaking his thigh, another his neck, and a boatswain's mate broke his collar-bone twice.

The storms were extremely trying for, although they forced the ships to lie-to under bare poles or a reefed mizen for days on end, there would be a sudden let-up, encouraging them to set double reefed courses and perhaps to increase with topsails.  Then without warning the wind would return, snow-laden and with redoubled violence, and tear the sails from the yards.  The rigging and sails would be frozen solid, easily snapped and broken.  The men, too, suffered severe frostbite while working aloft.  How they could work on the yards at all in such conditions is amazing. The old sailor's adage—'one hand for the ship and one for yourself'—was all very well but how could they do anything with both hands and feet frozen?

This sort of weather continued on and off whilst they made efforts to get westward. Great squalls and mountainous seas struck at them: the winds were extremely cold. On *Centurion* the main topsail split and one of the straps of the main dead-eyes broke, a serious mishap likely to be repeated unless it could be attended to quickly and this is what just could not be done. In the very high seas, which never ceased their onslaught, the ship began to grow loose in her upperworks and let in water at every seam. Every part of the ship was exposed to continuous drenching so that few, even of the officers, lay on dry bedding and were regularly driven from it by deluges.

*Centurion* was in trouble. A violent storm on 23rd March had the crew on the yard, trying to control the main topsail but the bolt rope at the foot broke and the sail split to ribbons blowing clean away. Anson signalled the fleet to bring-to, and then it was found that the topsail yard was also sprung. When the weather moderated, the yard was lowered for the carpenters to get to work upon it and to

*Anson put men in the shrouds to act as a wind vane*

repair the rigging.   This done, a new sail was bent and in quieter
weather they got under way again, but a more furious storm than
they had yet experienced hit them and all sail had once more to be
taken in.   The *Centurion* held her position better than the rest,
finding it necessary to manœuvre to avoid losing touch with them:
and, as it was impossible to carry sail, Anson put men in the shrouds
to act as a human wind vane to keep the ship's head off the wind—an
ingenious improvisation which did what was necessary but at the
cost of one of their best seamen lost overboard.   He was a good
swimmer: the fact that his mates were unable to help him made the
accident all the more tragic.

Eventually the violent gale blew itself out and a calm spell
followed.   It was accompanied by a thick fog during which a gun
had to be fired every half-hour in order to keep the Squadron
together.   On 31st March *Gloucester* fired a gun and made a signal
to speak to the Commodore.   The *Centurion* bore down to her and
discovered that *Gloucester*'s main-yard was broken in the slings—
that is exactly in the middle where the yard was supported by ropes
to the masthead—a very serious matter indeed.   The mainsail was
the biggest in the ship and its loss would mean that the Squadron
would be slowed in its progress.   Anson had carpenters from every
ship put on board the *Gloucester* to expedite the work of repair.

At the same time *Tryal* reported her pumps in such poor condition that the ship made more water than could be kept under.   A
spare pump from *Centurion* was sent over to her.   By a stroke of

*A pump sent to* Tryal

rare good luck these two repairing jobs were carried out in very moderate weather, boats being used for the journeys between the ships—a service that would have been impossible under the earlier conditions or those that were still to come.

On 1st April the weather deteriorated again and in a day or so had reached a pitch of violence even worse than any they had yet experienced. At the very beginning a sea burst upon the port quarter gallery of the *Centurion* smashing it in and inundating the ship. Once more the rigging suffered extensively: a main dead-eye strap broke and also a main shroud and futtock shroud. To prevent further trouble and to ease the strain upon the masts and shrouds, they lowered main and foreyards and lay-to in that condition for three days. Twenty-four hours' respite when the storms died away encouraged Anson to make sail again but the next day he had to repeat his safety measures whilst being punished by yet another gale with lightning and rain.

During the night several guns were heard firing to leeward—a signal of distress—and the Commodore made a signal for the Squadron to bring to. At daybreak they saw the *Wager* far to leeward of the other ships, her mizen mast and main topsail yard missing. *Centurion* immediately bore down to her and discovered that this disaster was due to the rottenness of her ironwork, all the chain plates to windward having given way when the ship rolled heavily. This was trouble enough, but on the following day the *Anna* pink made a signal of distress and on closing her and speaking to her master Anson heard that the pink's forestay was broken and also the gammoning of the bow-sprit.* This was extremely dangerous as all the masts might collapse so that it became imperative to put the ship before the wind. The whole Squadron had to accompany the pink until she had effected the necessary repairs when they were able to swing off on to their proper course again.

The expedition had now endured some forty days of terrible weather. In order to preserve their ships and their lives, the crews had been compelled to labour at full stretch without cessation and were in urgent need of rest. Anson hoped that conditions might at last improve as he reckoned that his Squadron was about 10° off the western tip of Tierra del Fuego—at least twice the distance thought by earlier navigators to be required to counteract the set of the eastward current. On this calculation the Squadron could safely turn to the north and, indeed, by mid-April they reached the latitude of the western entrance to the Straits of Magellan. But in the small hours of the night of the 14th in hazy weather, a break in the mist

---

* The gammoning was a strong lashing which bound the bowsprit to the stem-head.

4

revealed land right ahead about two miles off!   The fleet was hastily put about and twelve hours later had managed to put near 60 miles between the ships and the coast.   Anson was amazed that the current should have set them so far to the east with such strength as the Squadron should, in his reckoning, have been about 300 miles further west.

This narrow escape shattered Anson's hope of winning some relief for his exhausted men.   He had no alternative but to steer southward once again, as he dared not risk being set on that dangerous shore by the terrible westerlies; and yet the further south he went the worse the gales would surely become.   His crews were dispirited.   Men were falling sick and dying.   Moreover, the *Severn* and the *Pearl* which had slipped from sight one morning had not been found in the subsequent search; and the common belief was that both ships had run on shore.   With thoughts such as these the rest of the fleet stood away to the south-west wondering, after the recent experience, whether in the face of these tremendous westerlies they ever would be able to get clear of that fearful Cape.

*Gammoning of the bowsprit broken*

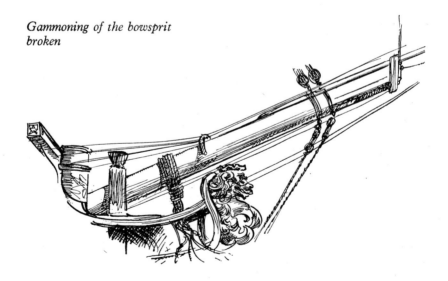

# 5

# *The Horn takes Toll*

AFTER TEN days of sailing southward the Squadron reached a latitude of about 60°S. During those ten days they enjoyed a respite from the storms; and, indeed, the weather was more cheerful than any they had encountered after clearing the Straits of Lemaire. But on 24th April, the wind strengthened and by the evening a terrific storm was battering them. The weather became very thick and *Centurion* lost sight of the other ships. In the morning, during an attempt to get the topsails on, the clue lines and bunt lines broke and, the sheets being slackened, every seam in them was split from top to bottom: the main topsail was thrashing so heavily that it smashed away the top lanthorn and threatened the head of the mast. Some of the most daring of the men at great risk to their lives went aloft to lay out on the yard to cut the sail away below the reefs. The fore topsail was whipping at the masthead with such fury that it was ripped to pieces and the mainsail then tore loose and both fore and main yards had to be lowered to confine the sails. *Centurion* lay-to under the mizen whilst her crew licked their wounds.

By noon of the next day they were able to raise the yards and undertake some of the essential rigging repairs. They saw nothing of the other ships of the Squadron and in fact continued entirely without any knowledge of them until after their arrival at Juan Fernandez in June. For the rest of April they endured hard gales but notwithstanding the weather they made slow but steady progress northward until by the end of the month they judged that they were in latitude 52°S and clear of Cape Horn. Hopes rose that at last they would have no more of the tempests that had made the last eight weeks of their lives a misery.

But Cape Horn had by no means finished with them, for what had gone before was to be far exceeded in terms of damage to ships and rigging and in sickness and death amongst the crew. Scurvy—the scourge of early voyagers—was first noticed soon after they had cleared the Straits of Lemaire. On 31st March Thomas wrote:

> And now as it were to add the finishing stroke to our misfortunes, our people began to be universally afflicted with the most terrible, obstinate, and at sea, incurable disease, the scurvy, which quickly made a most dreadful havoc among us, beginning at first to carry off two or three a day, but soon increasing and at last carrying off eight or ten; and as most of the living were very ill of the same distemper, and the little remainder who preserved their healths better, in a manner quite worn out with incessant labour, I have sometimes seen four or five dead bodies sewn up in their hammocks, others not, washing about the decks, for want of help to bury them in the sea.

Walter attributed the outbreak to fatigue and low-spiritedness amongst the men, but this, of course, we now know to be incorrect. He was surprised that it still carried off men even though the ships were getting northward. The death-roll from this sickness for April was forty-three and there was hardly anybody who was not affected by it in some degree. In May nearly twice as many died as in April, and by the middle of June over 200 men all told had died. Only six foremast hands capable of duty could be found in a watch.

*Men dying at the pumps*

Nowadays scurvy is practically unknown in the western world. Before the introduction of citrus drinks into their diet, the crews of ships on long voyages were particularly subject to this disease: and Walter left a detailed account of it, horrifying to modern readers.

It's symptoms are inconstant and innumerable, and its progress and effects extremely irregular; for scarcely any two persons have the same complaints and where there hath been found some conformity in the symptoms, the order of their appearance has been totally different. . . . The common appearances are large discoloured spots over the whole surface of the body, swelled legs, putrid gums, and above all, an extraordinary lassitude of the whole body, especially after any exercise, however inconsiderable. And this lassitude at last degenerates into a proneness to swoon on the least exertion of strength, or even the least motion.
. . . At other times, the whole body but more especially the legs, were subject to ulcers of the worst kind, attended with rotten bones, and such a luxuriancy of fungous flesh as yielded to no remedy. But a most extraordinary circumstance, and what would be scarcely credible upon any single evidence, is that the scars of wounds which had been for many years healed, were forced open again by this violent distemper: of this, there was a remarkable instance in one of the invalids on board the *Centurion*, who had been wounded above fifty years before at the Battle of the Boyne; for although he was cured soon after, and had continued well for a great number of years past, yet in his being attacked by Scurvy, his wounds, in the progress of his disease, broke out afresh, and appeared as if they had never been healed: Nay what is still more astonishing, the callous of a broken bone, which had been completely formed for a long time, was found to be hereby dissolved, and the fracture seemed as it had never been consolidated. Indeed, the effects of this disease were in almost every instance wonderful; for many of our people, though confined to their hammocks, appeared to have no inconsiderable share of health, for they ate and drank heartily, were cheerful, and talked with much seeming vigour, and with a loud strong tone of voice: and yet on their being the least moved, though it was only from one part of the ship to another, and that in their hammocks, they have died before they could well reach the deck: and it was no uncommon thing for those who were able to walk the deck and do some kind of duty, to drop down dead in an instant on any endeavour to act with their utmost vigour, many of our people having perished in this manner during the course of the voyage.

In this state then, with scurvy ravaging the crew, *Centurion* arrived on 8th May at the island of Socorro, which was the first rendezvous appointed in the Pacific. Anson cruised off-shore for several days. Having no charts of this part of the coast, and with a wind blowing strongly from the west, he could not afford with his debilitated crew to close the land and enter by one of the rocky openings visible from the sea. The risk of being driven on a lee shore, losing both ship and men, was all too obvious and Anson wisely decided to remain where he was. Disappointment was bitter. On Friday, 8th May, Thomas wrote:

> ... at seven in the morning, saw the mainland of Patagonia appearing in high mountains covered mostly with snow. We likewise saw several islands, one of which we took to be the Island del Soccoro, so called by Sir John Narborough, in his account of his voyage into those parts; and from the fine description this gentleman had given of this island (having been there in the very height of summer), this place was appointed for our first general rendezvous in the South Seas. An unhappy appointment it was in its consequences; for when the people, already reduced to the last extremity, found this to be the place of rendezvous, where they had hoped to meet the rest of their companions with joy, and what a miserable part of the world it appeared to be, their grief gave way to despair; they saw no end to their sufferings, nor any door open to their safety. Those who had hitherto been well and in heart, now full of despondency, fell down, sickened and died; and to sum up this melancholy part, I verily believe, that our touching on this coast, the long stay we made here, and our hindrance by cross winds which we should have avoided in a direct course to Juan Fernandez, lost us at least sixty or seventy of as stout and able men as any in the navy. This unspeakable distress was still more aggravated by the difficulties we found in working the ship, as the scurvy had by this time destroyed no less than 200 of our men, and had in some degree affected almost the whole crew.

They persisted thus for a fortnight, waiting for the remainder of the squadron and finding it more and more difficult to work the ship with their strength reduced by sickness to a dangerously low level.

*Cape Horn*
*greybeard*

The weather did not improve as Anson had hoped. Terrific squalls played havoc with the rigging and strained the masts. Had they been well clear of land they would have hove-to, but, as it was, they had great difficulty in keeping a safe offing with only their courses and topsails. As an additional hazard the *Centurion* was struck by lightning and several men and officers were burned.

Conditions became worse and worse. Harassed and driven by storms, and fighting to keep their ship in condition to carry on, they experienced a succession of disasters culminating in a hurricane on 22nd May. Nearly all the sails were split and most of their standing rigging broken. At eight in the evening, Walter says, 'a mountainous overgrown-sea took us upon our starboard quarter'. The great wall of water, known to later generations as a 'Cape Horn greybeard' from its smoking crest of foam, struck the *Centurion* and nearly finished her. Ballast and stores were shifted, a number of shrouds parted and the masts were in danger of going overboard. There were no sails left that were fit to send aloft, and in the hollow seas the violent rolling of the ship for want of sail to steady her frightened the hardiest sailors. But they could not give up—there was a murderous rocky coast under their lee—and by the combined efforts of the ablebodied and the convalescents the shrouds and sails were repaired after a fashion. The wind shifting to the southward, they steered away from the land under the mainsail only, with the Master and Walter managing the helm, and after two days found better weather than any they had encountered since the Straits of Lemaire.

Anson decided to take advantage of the improving weather and set course direct to Juan Fernandez. Although Baldivia on the mainland was scheduled as the next calling place, he thought that, as nothing had been seen of the rest of the Squadron, it was unlikely that they would be found there. By this time, indeed, he felt certain

that the others had come to an unfortunate end. Moreover, the
condition of his crew, the ship and the rigging, made it imperative
to reach a healthy spot where they could nurse the sick and refit undisturbed. His men were dying at the rate of four, five and six a
day so that he decided to press on to Juan Fernandez, planning to
sail, if possible, on the meridian, on which the island was marked on
the charts. They were unable to fetch it at the first attempt but
found the coast of Chile, on the same parallel. This gave them their
position and they stood to the west again: but what had taken two
days to sail eastward cost them nine to recover. Delayed by calms
and contrary winds and with their companions dying off like flies,
the survivors were the prey of terrible dejection aggravated by a
growing shortage of fresh water and the prospect of continuing at
sea. Only a few foremast men in a watch were fit for duty and some
of these were lame and unable to go aloft. In this condition they
arrived at the island of Juan Fernandez on 9th June.

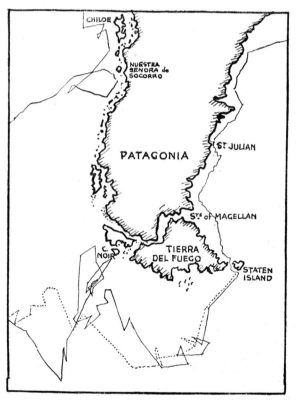

*Dotted line of Anson's presumed course*
*Solid line is his actual course*

# 6

# *Respite*

AT DAYBREAK they first saw Juan Fernandez about 35 miles off—in the words of Thomas, 'to our inexpressible joy having been from St. Catherine's, in the Brazils, to this place 148 days, on such a dreadful and fatal a passage as I believe very few persons ever experienced'. All that day and the following night they tried to close with the land but the men were so debilitated that the lieutenant of the watch could find only two quartermasters and six foremast men capable of working, and if the officers and servants and the boys had not lent a hand it is possible they might never have reached the island. Even then it took this poor band two hours to trim sails.

On the 10th they managed to get within 2 miles of the shore and sailed along the coast looking for their intended anchorage which was in the bay on the north side. At this distance the island presented the most luxurious appearance, a paradise of beautiful valleys and streams and woods. One can imagine how tense these men felt. Water was cascading down the rocks and there were green things in abundance. For the crew, living on a very short allowance of water, which by that time was crawling alive, the thought of getting their mouths to one of those springs must have driven them frantic with excitement.   The prospect of a spell ashore at such a place as this was almost beyond their dreams.   Indeed, when they were able to explore inland, they found most glorious woods and valleys, each with its clear sparkling stream tumbling through a classic landscape. Some spots there were where the shade and fragrance of the woods, the lofty and overhanging rocks presented scenes of such elegance and beauty which it would be difficult to match in any part of the world.

The Commodore later pitched his tent on a lawn half a mile from the sea from which he could observe, at the end of an avenue through the woods, his ships in the bay at anchor . . . which was probably the very spot on which Captain George Shelvocke* pitched his tent after his shipwreck on the island in May, 1720.   Shelvocke himself says: 'I now took some pains to find out a convenient place to set up my tent, and at length found a commodious spot of ground not half a mile from the sea, having a fine stream of water on each side, with trees close at hand for firing, and building our huts'.   Myrtle woods swept round behind the lawn: on rising ground and above them could be seen the high precipices inland which gave grandeur to the view: and two streams ran, one either side of the lawn.   It sounds a truly beautiful setting.

Those who were able, and there were few such, struggled to the deck to feast their eyes on this lovely picture.   They did not find their bay before nightfall and although the crew were all in, Anson cruised about keeping his distance from the shore.   But the dawn found them closer in, set by the current dangerously near to the shore and they had to let go their best bower anchor in 56 fathoms, about half a mile from the land.

At four in the morning the cutter was sent off in charge of the third lieutenant to find the bay.   Eight hours later he returned, his craft filled with seals and grass, which in the time available was the best food he was able to procure.   The grass was eagerly consumed and although the seals were not thought much of they were fresh meat.   At the same time those on board the *Centurion* had caught a fine quantity of fish.

The cutter had found the bay some distance along the coast and the next morning they prepared to weigh anchor and move on.   To

---

* Captain George Shelvocke, by his own account, began his career under Admiral Benbow and subsequently served in the Navy during the wars of William III and Queen Anne. In 1719 he commanded the *Speedwell*, a privateer, which in company with a larger ship sailed for the Pacific. He was wrecked on Juan Fernandez in 1720 and after many adventures returned to England in July, 1722. He was arrested for piracy soon after his arrival but was acquitted. Nevertheless he found it advisable to leave the country for France. He published his narrative in 1726.

such a degree of weakness were they reduced that it took four hours with all available men straining their utmost to get the cable up and down* and even then after putting on extra purchases to increase their power, they were unable to break the anchor out. One can guess at the agonising frustration and the frenzied futile exertions of the men around the capstan at this disappointment. But at noon a fresh breeze blew up and they were able to sail the anchor out and proceed on their way. When they arrived at the bay the wind suddenly shifted and blew from the land but they luffed up and sailed in until the dragging anchor fetched them up in 56 fathoms.

Thus did *Centurion* arrive at her first anchorage in the Pacific. She had come into that ocean three months previously with between 400 and 500 men almost all in reasonable health. They now numbered just over 200 out of which there were not enough capable people, even when officers, their servants and boys, were included, to work the ship in an emergency.

They had hardly settled in the anchorage when a sail was discovered standing into the bay. It could only be one of the Squadron and on closer approach it was clearly the *Tryal*. The *Centurion*, weak in manpower though she was, immediately sent some hands on board the sloop and they brought the smaller vessel to anchor between *Centurion* and the shore. The commander, Captain Saunders, came aboard and reported that only himself, his lieutenant and three of his men could work the ship. Out of his small complement he had buried thirty-four and all the rest were desperately ill with scurvy. On 24th April, the *Tryal* having separated from the rest of the fleet made her way as instructed to Nostra Señora del Socorro. The misfortunes which had dogged them were increasing and the effective crew were reduced by sickness to four or five men and a couple of boys and these few had to work the ship, mend and repair sails and rigging and bury the dead. Millechamp says that their chief food was bread toasted over burning brandy in order to kill the insects which infested it. They met the *Anna* pink but very soon lost sight of her again. Had the weather not improved somewhat it is possible that the *Tryal* would never have reached Juan Fernandez even with the repaired masts.

With what strength they could bring to bear they were now in great haste to get tents erected ashore for the sick. On board, men were dying fast. Walter says that without question this was partly due to the filth and stench on board, conditions arising from the

* To get the cable up and down meant that it was hove-in so far that the hawse-hole was directly above the anchor on the sea-bed.

great number lying sick and the impossibility of sparing the few who could work the sails to nurse them.

If Walter says stench and filthiness then the reader must infer the very foulest he can imagine and then more.   It requires some knowledge of what a clean ship was like in Anson's time to realise how a mildly dirty vessel would have stunk.   To start with, a ship had in her bilges a foetid solution commonly referred to as bilge water. The smell of this permeated the ship and could turn the stomach of anyone new to it.   Down below were stores of edibles—the provisions—slowly ageing and with a scent that was all their own. Above, hundreds of men, each allowed 14 to 15 inches of hammock space for sleeping.   These same men lived and slept in their clothes, such as they were, often soaking wet and certainly verminous.   It is only since the advent of modern insecticides that it has become possible to keep ships free from bugs and, in the overcrowded conditions of crews in Anson's time, they would be accepted without comment. People ashore could not keep free from them—in fact they were a part of everyday life.

Add to all this the state of things when virtually the whole crew were ill and a very great proportion were confined to their hammocks. Remember also that there were no sanitary arrangements on board —that buckets and pots were the only hospital furniture and surgical

*The Commodore pitched his tent on a lawn*

science was hardly born.    Consider the state of the lower deck in the
*Centurion* in bad weather.    All the gun ports were closed to keep
out the seas and that meant fresh air was also barred.    All the able
men were needed to work the ship, and sick men would have to do
what they could for themselves and each other.    There were few
men to spare for nursing duty.

Whilst Anson was battling his way in the Pacific Smollett sailed as
surgeon's mate in one of the ships of the Cartagena expedition.
What he experienced on that voyage he described in *Roderick Random*
and, though written as fiction, his account of life below decks is that
of an eyewitness, not a novelist.

> . . . I assisted Thomson in making up his prescriptions: but when
> I followed him with the medicines into the sick berth or hospital,
> and observed the Situations of the patients, I was much less sur-
> prised that people should die on board, than that any sick person
> should recover.   Here I saw about fifty miserable wretches,
> suspended in rows, so huddled one upon another, that not more
> than fourteen inches space was allotted for each with his bed and
> bedding: and deprived of the light of day, as well as of fresh air;
> breathing nothing but a noisome atmosphere of the morbid steams
> exhaling from their own excrements and diseased bodies, devoured
> with vermin hatched in the filth that surrounded them, and desti-
> tute of every convenience necessary for people in that helpless
> condition.
>
> I could not comprehend how it was possible for the attendants
> to come near those who hung on the inside towards the sides of the
> ships in order to assist them, as they seemed barricaded by those
> who lay on the outside, and entirely out of the reach of all visitation.
> Much less could I conceive how my friend Thomson would be
> able to administer clysters, that were ordered for some in that
> situation: when I saw him thrust his wig in his pocket, and strip
> himself to his waistcoat in a moment, then creep on all-fours
> under the hammocks of the sick, and, forcing up his bare pate

*Sighting Juan Fernandez*

between two, keep them asunder with one shoulder until he had done his duty . . .

We can only be amazed that men, as he said, could survive.

Anson's impatience to get the sick men moved was hindered by the lack of sufficient fit men to set up tents on the island, but at last on the 16th and for the next two days all the invalids were brought ashore, to the number of 167, not including twelve who died in the boats while being removed from the ship. Most of the sick men had to be carried in their hammocks at all stages as they were too ill to walk and, because there were so few to do the carrying, they had a rough time of it. Anson had no hesitation, therefore, in making all the officers without exception do their stint of this work and also did a share of it himself.

They had thought from their experience of scurvy and its treatment that in a very short time the green food and the excellent climate of Juan Fernandez would have had the sick men on their feet again. But the invalids continued to die at a great rate, rarely less than six a day. Those that recovered did so but very slowly and the only men to regain their health quickly were those who were strong enough to crawl about at their first arrival on shore.

Juan Fernandez had been written up sufficiently well by previous navigators for Anson to estimate how suitable it would be for the recovery of his men. Dampier, Shelvocke and Woodes Rogers* had all described its splendid climate and vegetation. The soil if accidentally turned was immediately overgrown with turnips and sicilian radishes. Anson had with him garden seeds and various fruit stones which he planted 'for the better accommodation of his countrymen who should hereafter touch here.' He planted lettuces, carrots and set in the woods a great variety of plum, apricot and peach stones which grew successfully.

Alexander Selkirk, the original of Defoe's *Robinson Crusoe*, during his four years on the island according to his account, killed 500 goats and after slitting the ears of a similar number, let them go free. Some of these marked animals were found by Anson's men thirty-two years after Selkirk had left the place. Goats were originally introduced into the island by Juan Fernando who attempted a settlement there with some families. When the Spaniards had conquered Chile they removed the whole colony to the mainland.

---

* William Dampier (1652–1715), buccaneer, circumnavigator, hydrographer and for a period captain in the Navy. He touched at Juan Fernandez on several occasions, the latest being in January, 1709, when he rescued Alexander Selkirk. Woodes Rogers (d. 1732), sea captain and governor of the Bahamas, commanded the expedition of 1709, Dampier serving as master of the *Duke*. Both Dampier and Rogers wrote accounts of their voyages.

There were no venomous or savage animals in the island but a few dogs and cats could still be found.

Anson's men were not fast enough to catch more than about one goat a day, but fortunately for them there were seals in plenty. Although at first they could not stomach seal flesh, the lack of any other fresh meat soon drove them to it and in the end they came to relish it and call it lamb.   Sea-lions were also eaten under the title of beef.   There was a magnificent supply of fish such as they had never before met.

The chief tasks to be tackled after the sick had been transported safely ashore were the cleansing of the ship, and the filling of the water-casks.   The first was an absolute necessity, as the decks were in a loathsome state due to the inability of the crew to clean them over the past weeks.   The filling of the casks was a job of some urgency in view of the possibility of enemy action.   There was evidence—ashes, fish bones and broken pots on the beach—that ships had been at the place very recently although Spanish mer-chantmen were advised not to touch there as it was a rendezvous for their enemies.   Anson did not know, of course, that Pizarro had returned to Buenos Aires, and there was also the chance that a force had been fitted out against him from Callao.   The *Centurion* in her present state would have been no match for even a small privateer as there were not more than thirty hands fit to work the ship and man the sixty guns.

Whilst the cleaning and watering were proceeding, a large copper-oven was set up near the tents and bread was baked every day for the ship's company in the hope that with the fresh fish and green produce they might recover their health the more speedily.   The possibility of some serious accident that in their helpless condition could easily overwhelm them was a continual worry to Anson. In fact on 30th June in a violent gust the *Centurion* parted her small bower cable and immediately swung off to her best bower anchor, which fortunately held and brought the ship up.   At the time there were only a dozen seamen on board, but a boat was sent to the shore to bring all the fit hands back.   The wind eased and the boat re-turned with the extra labour: the cable was hove-in and with another anchor bent to it they warped their way back to the anchorage and let go in 41 fathoms.   In spite of a diligent search they failed to recover the small bower anchor, which was a quite serious loss.

By the middle of July a number of the men were well on the road to complete recovery and the strongest were put to chopping wood. The others carried the billets one by one to the boats.   A forge was set up ashore and those smiths who were capable of working pro-ceeded to repair the broken chainplates and other rotten ironwork

Little progress could be made with rigging repairs as there was insufficient junk* to make spun-yarn. The *Gloucester* was known to have a large stock on board so that this particular work was delayed in the hope that she would soon appear. The sailmakers were installed in a tent to repair the old sails and make new ones.

The arrival of the *Tryal* at approximately the same time as *Centurion* aroused hopes that the remaining ships of the Squadron might have survived and would ultimately reach the rendezvous. But nearly a fortnight went by before they saw another vessel. Knowing what they had themselves suffered and how near they were to destruction before they landed at Juan Fernandez, there was obvious reason for their acute anxiety about the fate of their consorts. When a ship at last appeared they saw that she was under courses and main topsail only—the very picture of a ship that had taken a battering of the kind they had recently endured. Before she came close enough to be identified, a fog cut off visibility. When it lifted there was no sign of the unknown vessel and for the next five days the men ashore watched vainly for her return with mounting uneasiness. Shortage of water, sickness, damaged hull or rigging; all these troubles could have reduced this ship's crew to a state when it was beyond their power to bring their craft to harbour. To everybody's great relief on 26th June the *Gloucester*, as it proved to be, sailed once more towards the island.

Anson immediately sent off his boat to the newcomer. It was filled with fresh fish, water and vegetables which arrived none too soon, for *Gloucester*'s people were in desperate straits. Two-thirds of their original number had been buried at sea and of those left alive only the officers and their servants were able to do any duty. They had been on a short allowance of water for so long that within a day or so they must have died of thirst. The ship could not yet make the bay in the face of contrary winds and she stood backward and forward at a distance of 3 miles. Anson, realising what was happening, sent a second supply of provisions and water. Captain Mitchell held the crews of both this and the previous boat without whom he was now quite unable to work his ship.

For nearly a fortnight the *Gloucester* did her best to get inshore. On 9th July she was seen at a considerable distance sailing to the east but was soon lost to sight and not seen again for a week. Knowing their desperate need of water, Anson was seriously concerned for her men, but on 16th July she reappeared about 12 miles off making signals of distress. *Centurion*'s long-boat was immediately dis-

---

* Junk was old and worn rope cut up and unravelled and the bits used for many purposes including that of making spun-yarn; mats to take chafe; gaskets to confine the furled sails; pointing ropes, in fact any job where there was little or no tensile strain.

patched with water and provisions under strict instructions to return without fail, as this boat could not be spared. The next day the weather was stormy and the boat did not return, and for three more days those ashore were prey to their worst fears. Eventually the sails of the long-boat were seen. A cutter was sent to her assistance and in a few hours she was towed to the anchorage.

The long-boat brought off six of the *Gloucester*'s sick men, two of whom died in the boat before they reached the shore. Anson now learned particulars of the desperate plight of the *Gloucester*. She had hardly a man in good health apart from the crews of the *Centurion*'s two boats. The sick were dying daily and but for the water Anson sent to them all would by now be dead from thirst. *Gloucester*'s men were in the depths of despair. They had been trying for a month to fetch the bay and were no nearer to reaching their haven than when they first saw it. Whilst Anson was listening to this story *Gloucester* disappeared from sight once again, but it was not long before she unexpectedly sailed into the bay and within an hour was safely anchored, between the *Centurion* and the land.

If it had not been for Anson's assistance with provisions and men, every soul in the *Gloucester* must have perished. As it was, three-quarters of her crew were lost, less than eighty men surviving to set foot on Juan Fernandez. Once ashore, however, the convalescents made a quicker recovery than Anson's party had done and only a small number of them died.

Captain Mitchell reported that, after his ship was forced away by the winds, he had been driven as far as the island of Mas-a-fuera about 65 miles to the west of Juan Fernandez. He endeavoured to get a boat ashore for water, which he could see in abundance, but the winds and the surf prevented a landing. The boat returned laden with plenty of fish, however, which in their state was no mean load to pull. Mitchell's description of Mas-a-fuera differed from the accounts given by former voyagers, and he was of the opinion that the island might well possess a few good harbours. This interesting suggestion raised the possibility that one or more of the missing ships of the Squadron might have mistaken it for Juan Fernandez and put in to rest and refit there. Accordingly Anson decided to send the *Tryal* to examine the coastline of Mas-a-fuera. To expedite this operation some of the *Centurion*'s best hands were sent aboard the sloop to overhaul the rigging and to fit her out with stores and water and with whatever else was needed from *Centurion* or *Gloucester*. By 4th August *Tryal* was ready. She hardly got under way before the wind dropped and after being set dangerously close to shore and having all available boats to her aid she was towed into the bay and anchored for the night. Next morning with a fair breeze she set off.

Anson set all the able-bodied men to overhaul the *Gloucester*'s masts and rigging and, within a very short time, they discovered a spring in the foremast just above the partners. The carpenters were of the opinion that two fishes made from an anchor stock would make a satisfactory repair. In other directions also improvisation was the order of the day. Although the Squadron had taken far greater stocks of cordage and canvas to sea than was usual, supplies of these essential stores fell far short of actual requirements, so heavy had been the rate of consumption during the voyage. They used up all the junk and old shrouds to make cordage and then were forced to unlay a cable for running rigging: and, in spite of exercising every economy, they were only able to complete one suit of sails. Meanwhile, the progress of the sick men was disappointingly slow. In the belief that the change would speed recovery, Anson had the convalescents transferred from tents to wooden huts where they would live apart and in less crowded conditions.

The crews were generally employed in collecting foodstuffs, cutting wood, or making oil from sea-lion blubber. The last was very useful to them in lamps, mixed with pitch to pay the ship's sides or with wood ashes as a substitute for tallow to give the ship 'boot hose tops'.* Flour became another problem. A satisfactory oven had been built for baking bread on shore, but the main stores of flour were on the *Anna* pink which had not yet arrived and on the island supplies were running low. By the end of July Anson found himself obliged to ration bread and, in the course of surveying his supplies, made the unwelcome discovery that a former purser had neglected to take on large quantities of provisions which had been specifically ordered.

On Sunday, 16th August, at about noon, a sail appeared and everybody was taken from the land into the ships, a necessary precaution in view of their ignorance of the nationality of the vessel. She was thought by many to be the *Tryal* returned, but as she drew closer three masts proved that idea wrong. Then she was thought to be the *Pearl* and then the *Severn*. All doubts were dispelled at last when the vessel proved to be the *Anna* pink and she was able to come to anchor in the bay without mishap. Her arrival brought general relief—no more fears of provisions running short before they could

---

* Boot hose tops or boot topping was the scraping away from the ship's bottom just below the waterline of all the grass and slime and barnacles accumulated there and 'paying' or daubing it over with a mixture of tallow, sulphur, or lime and rosin. This gave the waterline area a smooth surface and when freshly done imparted a creamy-white colour.

reach a friendly port, a misfortune which could still put paid to the expedition. The men returned to a full allowance of bread. With *Anna* once more in the squadron, the whole company's spirits rose. Every man felt that the bad luck which had dogged the squadron must now be finished and began to look forward once again to meeting the Spaniards and their treasure ships.

*Sick men carried ashore*

66628

# 7

# *Adventures Recounted*

THE MEN of *Centurion* and *Gloucester*, still recovering from the effects of scurvy, were struck by the ease with which the *Anna* seemed to be handled. Two months had elapsed since their own arrival at Juan Fernandez, debilitated and in dire straits, and yet this ship and her crew appeared to be suffering no distress whatever. The explanation of this mystery, so they discovered, was that the *Anna* had been in harbour since the middle of May—a long period in which to recuperate from the hardships of rounding the Horn.

It will be remembered that the storm of 24th April, 1741, had scattered the Squadron. Thereafter the ships, except for *Severn* and *Pearl*, tried to make their way separately to one of the rendezvous appointed in Anson's original plan. On 16th May the *Anna* saw land about 12 miles off. They stood towards it but, their foresail splitting, they were unable to keep an offing and by the strength of the current were set towards the shore, where they dropped anchor in the lee of the island of Inchin. The crew, exhausted by incessant labour and scurvy, were too feeble to veer the cable fast enough and the ship drove towards the coast until after two days they were uncomfortably near to the inhospitable rugged crags against which the waves broke. The crew of sixteen men and boys gave themselves up for lost, thinking that even if by a miracle they should get safely ashore they would in all probability be murdered by the natives. To the local people any European was a Spaniard and would be treated as such. With such thoughts they drifted on until they came to a small opening in the land and, cutting away the two anchors which had been dragging all this time, they steered through it and found themselves in an excellent natural harbour where they came to anchor in 25 fathoms. This harbour is marked on maps to this day as Anna Pink Bay, and it lies below the southernmost island of the Chonos Archipelago and the peninsula of Tres Montes at about 45°30S on the west coast of Chile.

Here the *Anna* remained for two months. Ample supplies of fresh water, good provisions and rest effected a full recovery and put new heart into the men. The fierce Indians from whom they expected an attack did not materialise nor did the crew venture very far from their ship, but even had they done so it is highly improbable that they would have met any hostility, for the land behind the harbour was so mountainous and covered with forest as to be impenetrable.

The only people that they encountered during their stay at this place were an Indian with his wife and two small children. The Indian was travelling with most of his worldly possessions and Walter gives a list of them—a dog, a cat, a fish net, hatchet, knife, cradle, bark for roofing a hut, a reel, some worsted, a flint and steel, and a few roots which his family cooked for bread! The captain of the pink reasoned that if these Indians touched anywhere else along the coast, news of his whereabouts would leak out and so he took the precaution of keeping a gentle restraint upon them. In the daytime they came and went as they pleased in the ship, but at night they were locked in the fo'c'sle. They were fed and looked after well but, although the woman was quite content, the man became restless and after eight days he escaped with his family through a scuttle and to prevent pursuit he set the long-boat and his own periagua adrift. He rowed off in the *Anna*'s yawl and the watch on deck never heard a sound.

His departure revived their fears of being betrayed to the Spaniards. For the remainder of their stay, while the *Anna* was being got ready to resume the voyage, the master forbade the firing of the evening gun, which had been regularly observed since their arrival, and as soon as possible after the Indian's escape he put to sea with a restored ship and crew. The *Anna* made an uneventful passage to Juan Fernandez.

The *Anna* was the last ship to join Anson. The *Severn*, the *Pearl* and the store ship *Wager* had all gone missing soon after the Squadron arrived in the Pacific. The *Severn* and the *Pearl* lost contact

*Found themselves in an excellent natural harbour*

with the Admiral off Cape Noir and, as was afterwards learnt, they put back to Brazil. The *Wager* was unaccounted for. This ship was carrying some field guns together with some Coehorn mortars and a variety of weapons, tools and stores intended for land operations. As Baldivia was to be the place for the first attack, Captain Cheap was anxious that he should get his vessel to that rendezvous so that any delay in military operations should not be laid on his shoulders.

*Wager* therefore was making her way northwards as best she could and Captain Cheap decided, in view of the unlikelihood of any of the Squadron being at Socorro, to push on directly to Baldivia. They sighted land at about 47°S. The captain had to work hard to keep his ship clear of the dangerous coast and he had the misfortune to fall down the poop ladder and dislocate his shoulder, which left him temporarily incapable of command. The following morning the ship, which after the recent batterings was a near wreck, struck on a sunken rock and soon after was aground between two small islands.

*Wager* was perfectly safe where she was and the crew had only to wade a short distance to the shore, but a faction amongst them took to pillaging their vessel and arming themselves with whatever came to hand and threatening the rest of the crew. Some, as was to be expected, got at the spirit locker and in a foolish carouse managed to drown themselves in the 'tween decks where the water had flowed in. Cheap did his best to get his crew ashore, but had to leave the mutineers behind. Although he sent back the boats for them they would not come. Next day the weather became stormy and the ship seemed likely to break up, which put the mutineers in mind to get to

*The Indian and his family*

land, but the boat not coming straight away they fired a four-pounder at the hut where Cheap lay.

Discipline now began to fall to pieces. The necessary regulations for living under these conditions were flouted and each man was against his mate. The captain intended to fit up the boats and arm them for the voyage to Baldivia during which he fully hoped and expected to meet and take a Spanish vessel on the way. Even if they had no such success the boats were still well suited to get them to Baldivia. Most of the crew, however, were satisfied with the troubles they had already survived and were no longer interested in an enterprise which seemed so disastrous. Their idea was to lengthen the long-boat and make their way to Brazil through the Straits of Magellan and on to Great Britain, which was decidedly a much more dangerous proposition than Cheap's, but it smacked of going home and that blinded them to all argument. The captain tried unsuccessfully to get some sense into their heads, but they were out of hand and a young midshipman named Cozens, after a series of mutinous acts, was shot by Cheap and died fourteen days later.

Cheap's firm action subdued the men for a time, but by the middle of October when alterations to the long-boat were nearly completed the rebels used the death of Cozens as a pretext to confine the captain under a guard. They then sailed away in the long-boat, now converted into a schooner, and left Cheap and his party to do what they could with the yawl and the barge. At the time of the shipwreck there were 130 men on board *Wager*. More than thirty had died during their stay and eighty went off in the long-boat and the cutter to the south. Nineteen men were left behind—the maximum number that the barge and yawl could take.

On 13th October, five months after the shipwreck, the long-boat set out and eventually arrived at Rio Grande, on the coast of Brazil, on 29th January, 1742. On the way the mutineers lost a great many of their number from hunger and disappearance ashore at different places on the coast. Only thirty men survived to reach port. The cutter which was the only small boat they had with them had broken away and smashed. There was insufficient food and the loss of this boat frequently prevented them from getting ashore to replenish their water and look for provisions. But they made a remarkable voyage and the thirty survivors could count themselves very lucky men.*

* Sir John Barrow in his life of Anson says: '... it was in consequence of the mutinous and bad conduct of the shipwrecked seamen of the *Wager*, that Anson, in 1748, when he had the management of the Admiralty, in the absence of the Duke of Bedford and Lord Sandwich, got an act passed (21 George II) for extending the discipline of the navy to the crews of His Majesty's ships, wrecked, lost, or taken, and continuing to them their wages upon certain conditions'.

The captain and his small band prepared to voyage to the north-ward, but owing to bad weather and the difficulty of finding provisions it was two months after the long-boat had gone before they were able to get away. For they had been cast away, not upon the mainland as they imagined, but on an island at some distance from the mainland, that could provide them with nothing but fish, and a few green things. Wager Island was a small island just north of Wellington Island on the western coast of Patagonia, and divided from the peninsula of Tres Montes, to the north, by the gulf of Peñas. The mutineers had left very little of the ship's stores and this meagre supply had to be preserved against their coming journey.

All this time the *Anna* pink was not a hundred miles away—indeed probably not fifty—a fine roomy ship that could have had all *Wager*'s crew on board and carried them safely to Juan Fernandez.

On 14th December the captain and his party loaded the barge and yawl with all the provisions and pushed off. They had not been an hour at sea when a storm blew up that forced them to throw most of their supplies overboard to save themselves. They carried on, however, going ashore at intervals and picking up what food they could find. A fortnight later the yawl sank at anchor, drowning one of the men on her. The barge was too small to accommodate all the rest and they were forced to leave four marines behind on a desolate shore.

These four men were part of the detachment of invalids sent to Anson at the outset of his expedition. They were Corporal Crosslet

Wager *ashore*

and privates Smith, Hobbs and Hertford. When it became necessary for the barge to reduce its complement, these old men volunteered to be left at this unknown place to their certain death. They were soldiers, they said, and knew how to die. As the boat pulled away they cried 'God save the King' and by their action covered themselves and the Marines with glory. Such men will never be forgotten.

Cheap persisted in his courageous efforts to reach Baldivia, continually hampered by foul winds and accidents and having to interrupt his voyage to search for food.   By the end of January, 1742, after three abortive attempts to round a headland, he at last decided to give up the unequal fight and return to Wager Island where he arrived by the middle of February, hungry and disheartened.

His party was lucky enough to find some of *Wager*'s beef floating near the wreck which allayed their dreadful hunger and restored their spirits.   Two canoes with Indians aboard came to them, amongst whom was one who spoke a little Spanish.   The ship's surgeon, who knew the language too, bargained with this native to pilot the captain and crew in the barge to Chiloé, for which he should have the vessel in payment.

On 6th March the eleven people who now constituted the entire company set off on this new expedition.   A few days later, while Cheap and four of his officers were on shore, the remaining six and the Indian left in the barge, pushed off to sea and did not return.

The five men left behind were Captain Cheap, Mr. Hamilton, Lieutenant of Marines, the Hon. Mr. Byron and Mr. Campbell, Midshipmen, and Mr. Elliot the Surgeon.   Their case was desperate. They were on a desolate coast, with no food or the means of procuring it, no tools of any sort: they possessed, in fact, nothing but the rags they stood up in.   However, a short while after their marooning, the Indian and his family turned up in their canoe.   It appears that he had left the party in the care of another Indian while he went off a-fishing, but when he returned and found the barge gone and his companion missing he was convinced that the other Indian had been murdered.   When the survivors explained their critical position, he undertook to take them to a Spanish settlement and to provision them on the way.

*The four old
marines*

About the middle of March the little party set out in a convoy of Indians and canoes which their guide had organised. In a very short while Mr. Elliot the Surgeon died and the four survivors, after a complicated passage by land and water, arrived in the beginning of June at the island of Chiloé where the Spaniards treated them kindly. A whole year had elapsed since the *Wager* stranded in which time the ship's company had been reduced to four.

Captain Cheap was extremely weak and recovered with difficulty, and the others were in much the same case. Eventually, when they were well enough to travel, they were sent to Valparaiso and from there to St. Jago, the capital, where they stayed for over a year. Later Captain Cheap, Mr. Byron, and Mr. Hamilton were permitted to return to Europe on a French ship. The midshipman, Mr. Campbell, changed his religion and afterwards sailed with Pizarro to Spain in the *Asia*, where he applied unsuccessfully for a commission in the Spanish service. Having failed, he returned to England and had the astonishing effrontery to ask to be reinstated in the British Navy—a brazen application that was bluntly refused.

The story of the loss of the *Wager* and the disaffections of her crew does no credit to the people concerned. Several accounts of the adventures of the various parties were written, mostly intended to excuse the actions, rebellious and otherwise, which had been taken by their authors.

The first of these was by Bulkeley the Gunner and Cummins the Carpenter of the *Wager*, and was published in 1743. Mostly compiled from a log kept by Bulkeley, it explains the causes of the rebellion. At a Court of Enquiry held later both men were held not guilty of rebellion since from the time of the shipwreck they were not on the payroll and not therefore in the Navy. The Hon. John Byron, who finally threw in his lot with Captain Cheap, had wavered considerably before so doing. His story of the affair was published in 1768—twenty-seven years after the event, when he himself had become a commodore and by which time his memory of the episode could not have been too certain.

Walter says nothing of Bulkeley's journal. By the time he was writing, Bulkeley had already been acquitted and his readers could form their own opinions. A mutinous act of rebellion had been committed and the Court's decision was based on a technical point. It is better to remember the four old marines whose splendid sacrifice completely obscures the rather sordid chapter of excuses from the mutineers, justified in part though they may have been.

# 8

# First Blood

NOW THAT his men were recovered from scurvy, Anson was at last free to plan the next stage of his voyage and to weigh the resources available to him. Since leaving St. Helens *Centurion* had buried 292 men. Left on board were 214. *Gloucester* had buried the same number as the *Centurion* and had only eighty-two left alive. *Tryal*, with a somewhat better proportion, had thirty-nine living after burying forty-two. The poor old pensioners who had been sent on board at Portsmouth had suffered grievously, for of fifty originally in the *Centurion* there were only four left and *Gloucester* had lost every one. In *Centurion*, out of seventy-nine marines only eleven remained alive: in the *Gloucester* two out of forty-eight survived.

The three ships had left England with a combined total of 961 men. Between them they now had only 335 men and boys, a number insufficient for the proper manning of *Centurion* alone, but hopelessly inadequate for three ships.

Anson was anxious to learn Pizarro's whereabouts. The Spanish squadron, he surmised, must have suffered as much as his own, but Pizarro had every port open to him in this part of the world and would be given all possible help to refresh and refit. The British ships were in no condition to risk offensive action and the best that, in his estimation, they might accomplish would be to pick up a prize or two and make their way home, leaving the Spaniards to triumph over the misfortunes of their enemies.

About a week after the *Anna*'s arrival at Juan Fernandez the *Tryal* sloop returned from her tour around the island of Mas-a-fuera without having seen any other ships of the Squadron. Only one practicable harbour had been found and that not very convenient.

The last half of August was spent in unloading the provisions from *Anna* when it was discovered that a large portion of the cereals was mildewed and rotten owing to the water that the pink had taken in through her seams. Some of her casks had decayed and bags of provisions were soaked through. Having no further call on her services the Commodore sent to Mr. Gerrard, her master, notice of her discharge together with a certificate of the duration of her employment. It was up to the master of the *Anna* to go where he thought best for his owners but, instead of departing, he wrote formally to Anson that his ship was so rotten in every way that he would not like to proceed any further without a thorough refit and with this in view he requested that carpenters should survey the *Anna*. Anson immediately ordered some to the work, with instructions to be very exact in their report. This they produced next day.

*The Spaniard surprised at the* Tryal's *size*

It appeared that the pink had fourteen knees and twelve beams decayed and broken; one breast hook broken and another rotten: all her ironwork eaten away with rust, her spirketing and timbers falling apart; and, when they ripped off some of her sheathing, they found the wales and outside planking in a sorry state, and the bows and deck very leaky.   In their opinion the ship was seriously in need of a complete refit.   But it was not possible for such an undertaking to be put in hand because there was not sufficient wood and iron in the Squadron for the job.   The master then proposed, on behalf of the owners, that Anson should buy the pink for the use of the Squadron.   An inventory was taken.   In addition to stores the *Anna* contained a considerable amount of useful material which was greatly needed by the Squadron, and so Anson agreed to purchase the vessel for £300.   The pink was broken up and her crew sent to the *Gloucester*, which was the ship in most need of hands.   Afterwards, however, one or two moved to the *Centurion* in consequence of a difference with Gerrard.

September found them completing their preparations for the next stage of the expedition.   The foremast of the *Anna* was converted into a main mast for the *Tryal* and her mainmast was left ashore for the *Wager* to use as a mizen if she should ever reach the island. (When the *Wager* was last seen she had lost her mizen, and her main topsail yard.)   While the Squadron was occupied with these affairs, a ship appeared over the horizon.   Naturally, they hoped that she would prove to be one of their missing consorts, but the newcomer steered away without coming close enough to signal, from which it was generally thought she must be a Spaniard.   Anson feared that she had seen the tents ashore and he decided that an effort must be made to intercept her.

*Centurion* was almost ready to put to sea.   By five in the evening they had set up the rigging and bent on the sails.   There being no wind, all available boats were called on to tow her out of the bay, but what little wind there was soon gave out and the ship was be-calmed for the night.   On the morning of the 9th, there was no sight of the strange ship.   They hoisted every stitch of canvas and sailed in the direction which, it was presumed, the vessel had taken, but after two days the search was abandoned and *Centurion* put about for Juan Fernandez.   For three days they had only light winds and then, when a good breeze piped up, they suddenly saw a ship about 15 miles away on their weather bow.   They were soon after her, crowding on sail, and the other for her part bore down towards *Centurion* flying Spanish colours and making a signal as to a consort. When *Centurion* did not answer, the stranger stood away again. Round went the *Centurion* after her, certain now that this was one of

Pizarro's squadron. Overboard went the casks of water and provisions that stood in the way of the guns, and down came all the officers' cabins.

A thick haze nearly lost them their quarry, but it cleared in an hour or so to show them that they had closed the distance sufficiently to see that the chase was only a merchantman with not even a tier of guns. When near enough, Anson fired four shots into her rigging, at which she came round towards the *Centurion*, with all her sails slatting about because no man in her would go into the rigging where the shot came flying.

She was ordered alongside. Lieutenant Saumarez took possession and brought off the officers and passengers. Of the latter there were twenty-five, all terrified by thoughts of the cruel treatment which they expected to receive. Saumarez did his best to reassure them. The crew, black and white, numbered fifty-three. Their ship was the *Nuestra Señora del Monte Carmelo*, bound for Valparaiso under command of Don Manuel Zamora. The cargo was chiefly sugar and cloth. But of more importance were some wrought plate and twenty-three serons* of dollars, at that time worth about £17,786. The captured ship was of little value to the expedition. She was about 450 tons, and thirty-five years old; and she had cotton sails and bad rigging, three useless four-pounder guns and no small arms except a few pistols belonging to the passengers.

The most important result of the capture was that for the first time Anson learned to his satisfaction, of the size and destination of Pizarro's squadron and, heard that he had been forced back round the Horn with the loss of two of his largest ships. The best news was that in the previous May an embargo had been placed on all shipping in those seas because of the presence of the English. On receipt of Pizarro's account of his own troubles the Spanish authorities realised that Anson's ships must have undergone the same ordeal and, as nothing had been seen of them, they were assumed to have perished. Accordingly, the embargo had been lifted.

From letters on board the prize Anson realised how near his Squadron had come to annihilation. Pizarro had suggested to the Viceroy of Peru that some part of Anson's fleet might possibly have rounded the Horn into the South Sea. If this were so, he shrewdly pointed out that the English ships would be in a very weak condition, and therefore he advised the Viceroy to dispatch whatever force he could raise to the south in order to pick off the English ships singly.

---

* A seron or seroon was a packet made and used in Spanish America, consisting of a piece of raw bullock's hide, with the hair on and formed whilst wet into the shape of a small trunk and sewed together. At that time each must have held about £3,000.

The Viceroy acted quickly. Four ships sailed from Callao—one of fifty, two of forty, and one of twenty-four guns. Three of them patrolled off the Port of Concepción while one was stationed off Juan Fernandez and all four continued thus until 6th June when it was deemed impossible for the English still to be afloat. The Spanish fleet returned to Callao only a few days before Anson reached Fernandez. If Anson had made his landfall when first in the area instead of on the 9th, the battered *Centurion* with her debilitated crew must have fallen an easy prey to a healthy, well-armed enemy.* One further piece of information from his prize was of immense importance. The Spanish men-o'-war had suffered damage in a storm and were laid up for repairs in Callao. At least two months would be required, so it was said, before they could be in commission again.

Most of the prisoners and all the silver from the prize were taken on board the *Centurion* and that evening both ships made sail towards Fernandez where they arrived the next day. During the journey the Spaniards heard an account of Anson's epic passage round the Horn so that when they saw the *Tryal* at anchor they were astonished at the speed with which, as they thought, she had been built. For, after such a thrashing as the English had taken, it was easier for them to believe that *Tryal* had been built at Fernandez than to understand how such a tiny vessel could have come safely round the Horn through storms which had driven back the finest ships of Spain.

A more leisurely examination of the captured letters revealed that several merchantmen were bound from Callao to Valparaiso. Anson wasted no time. Chance had given him just the opportunity to profit when every hope of carrying out the original intention of the

---

* When the Viceroy sent the ships out from Callao to look for Anson their instructions were to kill every English man without distinction, so Thomas says. 'Those bloody orders our Spanish Prisoners themselves were very much ashamed of, and the rather as they were treated by us with all manner of Humanity.'

Anna *pink*
*broken up*

expedition seemed to have vanished. *Tryal* with an extra ten men from *Centurion* set out the next morning to cruise off Valparaiso. The Commodore, in the light of what he had learned, decided to divide his force and use the two parts on separate missions, a policy which would increase the chance of prizes and at the same time confuse the enemy as to his whereabouts and intentions.

With the devil-may-care exuberance of their breed the sailors forgot all their previous hardships and, with their minds on the treasures to be gained, set to with a will to complete the work of fitting out their ships. Four or five days saw all the water and firewood got on board. The prize was armed with four six-pounders, four four-pounders and two swivels which were taken out of the *Anna* pink. The *Gloucester* took on board six of the Spanish passengers and twenty-three seamen to supplement her crew. Captain Mitchell was ordered to cruise off the high land of Paita at a sufficient distance to avoid discovery and to remain on that station until he was joined by the Commodore. This would be when the ships at Callao should be fitted out, or upon the occasion of any other necessity. On 19th September *Centurion* and her prize left Juan Fernandez and went to join the *Tryal* at her station off Valparaiso. Things were looking up. With no likelihood of attack at sea by the Spaniards, all they needed was a fat prize or two to make the expedition profitable.

# 9

# *More Captures*

IT TOOK *Centurion* three days to get clear of Fernandez owing to light and contrary winds. On the night of 23rd September a breeze piped up and split their main topsail. The next morning, when the sail was repaired, two ships were sighted and the prize separated from *Centurion* in order to remove any ideas from Spanish minds that there were English cruisers in the vicinity. *Centurion* stood on under all sail. The larger of the two strange ships came steadily on, but her companion hung back. Anson had cleared his ship for action, and when *Centurion* was within pistol shot he ordered the master to hail the stranger in Spanish. The gunners stood by, their matches burning, when to the surprise of everyone they were answered in English by her commander, who was none other than Mr. Hughes of the *Tryal*. The merchantman was a prize taken a few days earlier and the vessel lagging in the distance was *Tryal*, her speed reduced on account of damage to her masts.

*Tryal* joined them shortly afterwards and Captain Saunders, her commander, came on board *Centurion* to make his report. He had, so he said, chased the Spanish vessel for thirty-six hours and at times thought he should never catch her. In the night the Spaniards closed their scuttles, covered all their windows and then changed course. This ruse would probably have succeeded but for the fact that one small chink of light betrayed them and *Tryal* was able to come within gun-shot. Captain Saunders fired a broadside. The Spanish did not shorten sail at once but when *Tryal* made ready to give them another broadside, they submitted. Like the *Centurion*'s prize, the *Carmelo*, the *Arranzazu* was bound for Valparaiso, with a similar cargo except that the silver she carried amounted to only £5,000. She was exceptionally large for those seas being of some 600 tons.

In the course of the long chase the *Tryal* had run into trouble. Her mainmast was sprung and her main topmast had broken at the cap, and now when the little fleet of four ships was standing east-

66

ward she sprung her foremast as well and in consequence had no mast fit to carry sail. To add to this misfortune, the wind freshened to such an extent that the other ships were unable to lend her a hand and, as she could not be left, they had to stand by her for the next forty-eight hours. All the while they were drifting to lee-ward of their station at the very time they could expect enemy ships to be in the area.

The weather moderated on the 27th and Anson sent for the cap-tain of the *Tryal* who, when he arrived on board, handed the Commodore a paper detailing a whole list of defects from which the *Tryal* was suffering. Dismasted and leaking so badly that the pumps could hardly free her even with men working at them twenty-four hours a day, she was a menace to the lives of all aboard her. They petitioned the Commodore to take some measures for their safety, which, however, it was impossible for him to do. There were neither spare masts nor rope for rigging. There was no haven open to them on that coast for careening and repairing the leaks; nor, indeed, could they have spared the time for such work. Anson felt that the wisest course would be to transfer her crew and send her to the bottom.

*Tryal*'s prize, which had served in her time as a Peruvian man-o'-war, was to take *Tryal*'s place. She was to be manned by *Tryal*'s crew, whose officers were to be re-commissioned, and to be armed with twenty guns—twelve of *Tryal*'s and eight that had belonged to the *Anna*. Everything of use—arms, stores, ammunition, and any materials needed by the other ships—was to be taken out of *Tryal*, after which she would be scuttled and sunk. Anson instructed Captain Saunders, after making sure that *Tryal* was destroyed, to take his new command—now renamed *Tryal's Prize*—to cruise off the highlands of Valparaiso at a distance of about 40 miles. The *Carmelo*, captured by the *Centurion* and now under Lieutenant Saumarez, was to keep company with *Tryal's Prize* to assist in un-loading the *Tryal* and thereafter to join in the watch for merchant-men. Anson was especially anxious to prevent any news reaching Callao of the English being in those seas, and to ensure that no Spanish ship should slip by unnoticed. On 27th September, the Commodore went south to cruise to windward of Valparaiso.

Anson was satisfied that he had made the best use of his small force. The *Gloucester* was off Paita and the rest of his Squadron so stationed as to ensure, as far as possible, that any vessel working between Peru and Chile in the south, or Peru and Panama in the north, would be intercepted. Unfortunately these careful dis-positions proved valueless. He had ordered *Tryal's Prize* to cruise on station for twenty-four days and then to proceed to Pisco where

*Anson*

she would rendezvous with Anson. For several weeks *Centurion* cruised without sighting a single ship and eventually, after an equally unsuccessful attempt to join *Tryal's Prize* and *Carmelo*, both of which had disappeared, Anson set a course direct for Pisco. Here again he found nothing. It was not until 2nd November that both his missing ships came into view together. Captain Saunders told Anson that it was only on 4th October that he finally cleared the

*Tryal* and sank her.    The operation started in bad weather and the *Tryal*—without masts—rolled and pitched to such an extent that Saunders could not lay a boat alongside her.    During this time, they were all driven so far to the north-west that it became impossible to get back on station at the prescribed time.

Anson strongly suspected that the enemy must have got wind of their presence and had placed an embargo on all ships in the neighbourhood.    If this were the case, it was also logical to assume that the Spaniards were fitting out men-o'-war to bring the English squadron to action.    Their communications system was slow.    A message expressed from Valparaiso required a month to reach Lima but already fifty days had elapsed since the *Centurion* had made her first capture, so that on every count it was reasonable to suppose that the enemy was thoroughly alerted.    Accordingly, Anson planned to join the *Gloucester* off Paita where with his fleet united he would be in a position to give any ships from Callao a warm reception.    The Squadron kept a good distance from the coast to avoid discovery. All Spanish ships, as he knew, were under strict instructions to stop at Callao so that if the English ships had been seen they would have at once been recognised as enemies.

By 5th November, the Squadron was about 25 miles off the coast near Barranca, when a ship was sighted.    *Centurion* soon outsailed the prizes and after a chase of some hours came within range of the Spaniard, fired fourteen shots, and had the satisfaction of seeing the enemy lower his colours.    The third Lieutenant, Mr. Dennis, and sixteen men, took possession of the vessel—named *Santa Teresa de Jesus*—and the prisoners taken from her were sent back to *Centurion*. This new prize was a ship of some 300 tons, laden with timber, cocoa, coconuts, tobacco, hides, thread, cloth, wax, in fact a nice domestic cargo: but unfortunately, only about £170 in small silver money.    Valuable though this cargo was, it was useless to Anson, his only satisfaction in the capture being that it was a loss to the enemy.    After all, it was part of his commission to cause as much damage as possible to the Spanish trade in the Pacific.

The crew of this ship numbered forty-five.    The passengers, of whom there were ten, included a mother and her two daughters. This worthy lady, terrified by the stories of English brutality being circulated by the authorities, hid herself and her family below decks where in due course they were discovered by the boarding party. Dennis had the greatest difficulty in coaxing them to come out and even then all his diplomacy was required to dispel their fears of instant death or worse.    Anson on hearing of the affair ordered them to remain in their own quarters on their ship and live exactly as before.    To ensure their privacy he arranged that the pilot, who in the Spanish ships was generally the second most important person on board, should act as their guardian.

After this capture, Anson waited for the *Carmelo* and *Tryal's Prize* to come up with him, firing guns and making false fires every half-hour during the night. But the two ships were so far astern that it was daylight before they joined him. Anson's Squadron of four ships now proceeded to the north. Some of the cargo of timber on the latest capture was used to repair the boats and to mount swivel-guns in the bows of both the barge and pinnace that they might be properly armed for subsequent actions in which they would most certainly take part.

On 11th November, 1741, having arrived in the vicinity of *Gloucester*'s appointed station they sailed quietly around keeping a good look-out to avoid missing her. A sail was spied, chased and identified as Spanish. But the wind dropped and Anson ordered his barge and pinnace and *Tryal*'s pinnace, manned and armed to board the chase. At nine o'clock in the morning, Lieutenant Brett commanding, the barge ran alongside the merchantman and fired a volley of small shot just over the heads of the people on board, and before they had time to recover clambered over her rail with most of his men. The enemy, scared by the volley and the flashing cutlasses, capitulated on the instant. Brett had the sails trimmed and bore

*The Spanish lady and her daughters*

away for the *Centurion*, picking up the two pinnaces as he went. When about 4 miles from her he set off in the barge taking a number of the prisoners with him to give their information to Anson as quickly as possible.

This latest capture was of about 270 tons: on board were forty-three sailors and a mixed cargo of steel, iron, wax, pepper, cedar wood, plank, snuff, rosaries, European bale goods, powder blue, cinnamon, and 'Romish indulgences'! Although this cargo was practically useless to them, yet the ship was the best capture they had so far made for she was worth 400,000 dollars to the Spanish. She had left Paita about twenty-four hours previously after provisioning and watering and was now bound for Callao. She was named *Nuestra Senora del Carmin*.

The news which Brett was so anxious that Anson should hear was that a vessel had entered Paita a few days previously and reported to the Governor that she had been chased by a large ship which the master presumed to have been English owing to her size and the colour of her sails. This ship Anson correctly guessed to be the *Gloucester*, and her sails, like those on the other English ships, must by now have been very dirty and discoloured whereas the Spanish vessels would have whiter cotton sails.

The Governor of Paita upon hearing the story from the Spanish captain had sent word immediately to the Viceroy at Lima. The Royal Officer residing at Paita, in expectation of the English Squadron descending upon the town, was now hurriedly removing the King's Treasure, and his own, to the town of Piura about 40 miles inland. From his prisoners Anson also learnt that there was a considerable sum in cash—according to Thomas 400,000 dollars, belonging to some Lima merchants—now stored in the Custom House waiting to be shipped on board a vessel lying in the port. This ship was considered a fine fast vessel and was preparing to sail for the bay of Sonsonnate on the coast of Mexico to purchase part of the cargo of the Manilla Galleon.

The prisoners thought that the urgency with which her fitting-out had been forwarded would enable her to sail the next morning. The Commodore, having in mind the state of the *Centurion* after two years at sea, thought little of his chances of catching this slippery customer if once she put to sea. His obvious course was to attack Paita before the treasure could be removed, and this he decided to do at once.

*Paita burns*

# PART THREE
# Pacific Campaign

# 10

# The Sack of Paita

THE COMMODORE calculated that little danger to his Squadron could come from an assault on the town of Paita. Such an attack constituted the one offensive operation that in its present condition the little fleet could undertake with any hope of success, and it was unlikely to occasion any serious loss of life to his party. Moreover, his ships were overburdened with prisoners who were consuming too great a proportion of provisions from their heavily depleted stocks: and these 'useless mouths' could well be landed and left ashore.

The plan of Paita given in the original edition of Walter's book shows a small township which contained only 200 families. These families were mostly those of Indians and black slaves with some half-castes and a very few whites. Their houses were of one floor: built of wattle and daub and thatched with leaves—a simple architectural style which was perfectly adequate in a climate where rain was practically unknown. The port, if such it could be called, was a small bay which was at that time considered to offer the best anchorage in the vicinity. There was a regular traffic of merchant ships sailing from Acapulco, Sonsonnate, Realijo and Panama to Callao, usually in the teeth of strong winds, and they called at this town for water and provisions. In consequence of the discomfort of the sea voyage many travellers on these vessels disembarked here and finished their journey to Lima by a coastal road which had stations and villages along it for their accommodation.

Paita itself produced no foodstuffs or water, as was only to be expected in a place where rain was almost a curiosity. All such

necessities had to be imported into the town and were in fact brought
by sea from a place called Colan a few miles to the north. The locals
thought the water thus procured to be excellent stuff because it
flowed through woods of sarsaparilla with a consequent medicinal
quality. After sampling it, the English thought differently.

The boats in which the goods were brought along the coast were
'balsas', as Walter called them. This is a type whose origins are
lost in the distant past. Variations of it are found all over the world,
but from what is known of them, those that were referred to in
Walter's book were large cargo rafts which could have made the
passage in reasonable safety. Balsas, however, were basically of a
particular construction. Bundles of 'totora' reeds were bound together in boat form: in the smaller craft three bundles sufficed—
one for the bottom and one for each side. In the larger boats more
bundles were used and sometimes as in these Paita carriers a raft
shape was adopted. On them was a bipod mast, a yard for the sail,
and one or two beams to strengthen the boat—all of which would be
made of bamboo. The sail was of totora matting. The life of the
balsas was only two or three months, because the reeds became
waterlogged and quickly rotted.

The Commodore's decision to attack Paita was encouraged by the
further intelligence from his prisoners that the fort was a mere brick
shell with no ditch or outlying earthworks and armed with only eight
guns— four- and six-pounders. There was a small garrison—a
rather weak company which could be supplemented by about 300
men raised in the town. Accordingly Anson settled to attack the
same night and to use the ships' boats for the job. Paita was a small
place and it was unnecessary to employ the full strength of the

*Balsas*

Squadron.   The fleet was now about 12 leagues from the shore and it was thought wise to keep the ships out of sight of land.

The *Centurion*'s eighteen-oared barge and the *Tryal*'s and *Centurion*'s pinnaces were therefore manned with fifty-eight picked men under the command of Lieutenant Brett.   Two of the captured Spanish pilots were to go with the party to point out the best landing place and to act as their guides in the town.   Anson told all his prisoners that they would be released and set on shore at Paita if the two pilots did what was required of them, but if there was any treachery on their part they would be shot instantly and all the prisoners taken to England.

During the day the ships stood in towards the land and by ten o'clock they had reached to within 15 miles of Paita and at this point the boats put off.   Their journey to the land was not discovered until they entered the bay, when the crew of a Spanish vessel saw them and raised a hullabaloo.   The Spanish sailors jumped into a boat and rowed for the shore, rousing the town with their shouts.

Brett's men pulled hard for the beach, endeavouring to arrive before the Spaniards had time to put their defences in order.   But by now the men in the fort had a gun loaded, and as the English boats grounded, a shot flew over their heads.   With this encouragement they had virtually completed their disembarkation by the time that the second shot arrived.   Led by one of the pilots they rushed up the beach to the safety of a narrow street where they were sheltered from the fire from the fort.   Forming up as best they could in the short time available, they marched for the fort and the Governor's house in the Town Square.   The sailors whooped and yelled with

*The tars in ladies' gowns*

joy, for this was the first time they had been ashore in enemy terri-
tory since the commencement of the cruise, and their heads were
full of notions of a splendid pillage.  What with the banging of
drums, the shouting and general uproar in the middle of the night,
the inhabitants, who had been so rudely awakened, fully believed
that they were being attacked by a force of at least 300.   It was not
surprising therefore that the citizens with one accord concentrated
on getting away from the town as fast as possible.

As the attacking party entered the square, they were greeted by a
volley of musketry from the Governor's house.   The merchants
who owned the treasure that was stored in the Custom House, of
which Anson was proposing to relieve them, made some effort to protect their property.   They formed up on the gallery running round
the house as the most advantageous position for the defence of the
place.   But when the sailors returned their fire the merchants
followed the example of the rest of the people and cleared out with all
speed.

Brett now split his party into two.   One section was to capture
the Governor and the other to subdue the fort.   The Spaniards
in the fort had no more stomach for fighting than the townsfolk and
they beat a hasty retreat over the walls.   Brett, who was in charge of
this party, entered without opposition and thereby completed his
capture of the town within a quarter of an hour of his arrival on shore.
His only casualties were one man killed and two wounded, of whom
one was the Spanish pilot of the *Teresa*—the *Centurion*'s last prize.
Another casualty which Walter mentioned was that of the Hon. Mr.
Keppel's jockey cap,* the peak of which was shaved off close to that
gentleman's temple by a musket ball.

Having gained Paita, Brett placed guards at the fort, the Governor's house and around the town to prevent any surprise attack by
the enemy and ensure that nothing of the booty was stolen.   He
seized the Custom House where the bullion was stored and then
turned his attention to the people still remaining in the town.   But
there were very few left behind, the majority having decamped in
such a rush that they had not even had time to dress.   Most of them
were in bed when the English arrived.   The Governor was well to
the fore in this scramble.   He had been married three days before to
a young seventeen-year-old girl and yet at the first alarm he left her

---

* This jockey cap was not the parti-coloured silk headgear familiar nowadays on the
race-course.   The idea of a jockey cap on a sailor seems a bit odd, but there are contemporary pictures to prove that caps of this shape were used by all sorts of people on
land and water.   Those, at least at sea, seem to have been made of leather or stiffened
canvas.   The peak was sometimes turned up and sometimes worn at the back.   One of
the best contemporary pictures shows a member of Anson's barge crew wearing uniform which included a jockey cap.

to shift for herself and rushed half-naked from his house. His escape was to prove a source of trouble for Anson, who had planned to use him as a hostage in negotiating a ransom for the town.

Those residents who had not made their escape were confined in one of the two churches in the town under the eye of a guard. Some negroes who had fallen into the hands of the English were also set to work carrying the cash from the Custom House and other places to the fort, under the surveillance of a party of musketeers, and for the rest of the night the collection and sorting of the booty was the main interest of the conquerors. In the course of it the seamen indulged in some looting on their own account and soon came on the clothes left behind by the Spaniards in their rush for safety. Some of these were splendid garments, elaborately laced and embroidered in the fashion of this part of the world. In less than no time the sailors had them on their own backs over their dirty rags and, complete with bag wigs and magnificent hats, they patrolled the streets in high spirits. The tars who came later were no less delighted with the women's dresses and when Brett met a party of them he was not sure that they were his men.

Meanwhile Anson's ships having stayed below the horizon until one o'clock in the morning made sail for the bay where they arrived six hours later. To their great joy they espied the English flag flying above the fort and at eleven o'clock the *Tryal*'s boat came out to them filled with dollars and church plate. In the afternoon the ships dropped anchor about a mile and a half from the town, near enough to be within easy support of those on shore.

Whilst Brett was busy with his treasure, the townsfolk had been joined by numbers of people from outlying districts, and a large crowd assembled on a hill at the back of the town. They were reinforced by about 200 horsemen with trumpets, drums and flags, and to all appearances well armed and well trained. They paraded up and down on the hill, blowing their trumpets and banging the drums, and generally making a show to frighten what they now knew to be the very small number of their opponents. The sailors were not impressed, being well aware that no cavalry in its senses would venture into the narrow streets and houses to fight men on foot. So that Brett was able to carry on working undisturbed, transferring treasure and provisions to the ships as long as daylight lasted. As a safeguard against night attacks, Anson sent a reinforcement ashore with instructions to cover all the streets leading to the square and to erect barricades across them. But nothing occurred during the night and at daybreak work was resumed on loading the boats.

The unlucky effect of the Governor's escape from capture was becoming hourly more apparent. As the search parties combed the town, more and more wealth came to light and it was impossible to find room for all of it in the ships. If the landing party had managed to seize the Governor as planned, he would undoubtedly have been only too pleased to arrange for a ransom of the whole town, which would have suited both sides. But the Governor was free. It was due to his efforts that the menacing crowd of refugees from Paita and men from the surrounding countryside were assembled on the hill overlooking the town and he it was who had summoned the cavalry from Piura, 14 leagues away. Delighted by his success he had not the slightest intention of negotiating, whatever the consequences to the unhappy citizens.

Anson sent several messages to him suggesting that His Excellency might enter into a treaty for the ransom of the town and property, pointing out that a strict valuation and equality of exchange would not be insisted upon. Some livestock and necessary provisions for the Squadron would satisfy Anson. The Governor ignored all messages although the Commodore made it quite clear that, if his requests were not complied with, he would burn Paita and its contents to ashes.

Notwithstanding the Governor's arrogance and the bombast of his horsemen, the Spaniards were in trouble. A number of negro slaves deserted to the English; and others were found creeping into the town and carrying jars of precious water back to their masters on the hill. Hunger and thirst were becoming serious problems for the refugees, and it was easy to guess who had the water thus obtained. From the prisoners and slaves Anson learned that the Spanish were being increased to a large force. Under the lead of a Scotch Papist named Gordon, the captain of a local ship, they had decided to attack the English in the town the following night. Unperturbed by this information the sailors carried on with the shipment of treasure, but in the evening reinforcements were again landed as a precaution and the guards doubled at the barricades. The posts

*The Spaniards halted*

were manned by sentinels within call of each other and, to remove
any doubt in Spanish minds about the vigilance of the defence, they
beat the bounds with a drum at intervals until dawn.    This display
was sufficient.    The second night was as quiet as the first.

By 15th November Anson was ready to sail.    The captured pilots
had served him well and so, in fulfilment of his promise to them, he
sent his eighty-eight prisoners ashore.    Mr. Brett was told to place
them under close guard in one of the churches until he was ready to
embark his men.    The two churches were at a short distance from
any other building and, as Brett's last duty was to fire the whole
place with the exception of these churches, it was reckoned the
prisoners would be safe from the flames.

There were good stocks of pitch and tar in the town to start the
fire and the sailors spread the stuff in houses and stores so that the
fire would engulf as large an area as possible in the shortest time.
With luck the enemy would be unable to contain or suppress the
conflagration.    All being ready, Brett ordered the guns of the fort
to be spiked and then the fires were lit on the windward side of the
town.    When the flames had taken a good hold, the Lieutenant
collected his men together and marched to the beach at an open
place outside the town.    The Spaniards, seeing what was now
afoot, determined to hasten the departure of their tormentors and
get some honour out of the business.    About sixty of their best

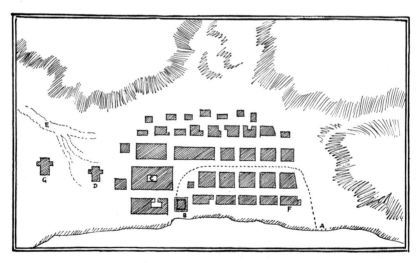

*The Town of Paita*
*dotted line shows route from A the*
*landing place: B the fort: C the Governor's house*
*D church: E road to Colan: F the treasure house:*
*G Monastery*

horsemen rode down the hill with a fine aggressive bearing and had the English not already sampled the courage of the local warriors they could reasonably have expected to be cut down on the open beach. As it was, Brett simply ordered his men to halt and face about, and the horsemen came to an abrupt stop and would advance no further.

The safe arrival at the beach was marred by the discovery that one of their number was missing. No one knew where he was or what had happened to him and after a short delay Brett decided that he could wait no longer. All the men were embarked and just pushing off when the missing man was heard calling to be taken in. The smoke from the fires was so thick that he was fortunate to be seen and picked up, for the water was up to his chin. It appeared that he had that morning drunk a stiff brandy and fallen into a heavy sleep from which he awoke only when the flames reached him. These and the sight of some Indians and Spaniards not far off sobered him fast enough and making his way through the thickest of the smoke he came to the water's edge and rushing into the waves was finally brought to a halt by his inability to swim.

I have a note in my copy of the original edition of an item in the *Gentleman's Magazine* of 1790:

At Sheffield after a short indisposition aged about 87, John Holme a sailor who went round the world both with Anson and Byron, being impressed into those hazardous services. He says he was the man whom Anson's voyage reports to have had so narrow an escape at Paita owing to his being drunk and for which he received a severe caution and could never after gain a naval promotion though he was then upon a level with Mr. Keppel (afterward the Admiral). He confirms the report of the gigantic size of the Patagonians. Though he had never seen any of them measured he considered that the common height was seven feet and some eight feet which is the height of their Queen. In a run from Gibralter to Malaga he was taken by the Algerines where he was kept in slavery for eighteen months from which he was redeemed by one of the Levanters.

After spending forty years in naval service he was admitted into Greenwich Hospital but his stay did not last long. By some irregularity in the accounts he got the slow boat, an indignity he could not brook so he ran off. He then journeyed to Sheffield and assumed the occupation of a cutler and married. He supported himself in comfort until about six weeks ago.

This remarkable character was the only man at Paita to get drunk on duty. Yet there was a vast quantity of liquor had the men decided to indulge, and considering their long isolation on board ship they exercised a wonderful self-control. Anson and his officers had disciplined them well.

7

The Spaniards now flocked down the hill in an effort to prevent
the fires getting too great a hold, but they were unsuccessful and
Paita with all the merchandise remaining in it was completely destroyed.    Brett with his party returned safely and Anson prepared to
leave that same evening.    On their first arrival in the bay they had
found six vessels at anchor.    The ship which was reported as the one
chosen to transport the treasure looked sound to Anson and he
decided to commandeer it for his Squadron.    The other craft consisted of a bark, two snows and two row-galleys of thirty-six oars
each.    These last were two of a fleet that had been built at various
places on the coast for the express purpose of preventing the English
landing to attack Lima, as the Spaniards had presumed Anson would
do ever since they first heard of his setting out.    Having no use for
these five craft the Commodore had them towed out of the harbour
and sunk.

This treasure transport, called *Solidad*, was given a crew of ten
men under command of Lieutenant Hughes of the *Tryal* and the
Squadron now numbering six ships sailed from Paita.    The booty
which they took with them constituted a mere fraction of the mass of
valuable material which was stored in the town.    They could only
guess the worth of it all.    For their part the Spaniards estimated
their entire loss at something like a million and a half dollars.    Pascoe
Thomas in his account says that the property burnt in the town
consisted chiefly of 'rich brocades, laced cloths, bales of fine linens
and woollens, britannias, stays and the like'; the plate and coin taken
amounted to over £30,000 in addition to jewellery and trinkets whose
worth was not ascertainable at the time.

One important result emerged from this action.    Anson had kept
his word and released his prisoners.    This, coupled with his humane
treatment of them when they were first captured, had made a pro-
found impression on people who had expected to spend the rest of
their lives in a cruel captivity.    The Spanish ecclesiastics had made
a good job of filling their countrymen with ideas of the barbaric
English, but their short time in Anson's power had been 'sufficient
to prove the friars liars' and all the prisoners left the Commodore
with strong assurances of their grateful remembrance of him.
Later on, English prisoners in the hands of the Spanish in all parts of
their empire were to reap the benefits of Anson's kindness.    They,
in their turn, were kindly treated by their captors which can in part
be attributed to Anson's conduct.

Byron, who with Captain Cheap and the other officers of the
*Wager* whilst a prisoner on parole in Chile, met some of these
released captives and he said: 'They all spoke in the highest terms of
the kind treatment they had received; and some of them told us

they were so happy on board the *Centurion*, that they would not have been sorry if the Commodore had taken them with him to England'. Surely no finer compliment could be paid to one's gaoler!

Although there was some criticism of the burning of Paita as a cruel injury to a hard-working community—Lord Stanhope thought that the act 'has imprinted a deep blot on the glory of Lord Anson's expedition'—Captain Basil Hall, R.N., visiting this area in 1821, held a different opinion.   He wrote: 'Lord Anson's proceedings are still traditionally known at Paita and it is curious to observe that the kindness with which that sagacious officer invariably treated his Spanish prisoners is, at the distance of eighty years, better known and more dwelt upon by the inhabitants of Paita than the capture and wanton destruction of the town'.

*The argument over the captured treasure*

# 11

# A New Plan

THEY LEFT Paita about midnight on 16th November, and at daylight Anson ordered the Squadron to spread out in order to find the *Gloucester*. Only one thing spoilt the general content at the outcome of their exploit. Men being what they are and sailors no better than the rest, a heated argument had broken out over the retention of the plunder taken by the shore party. The men who remained on board the ships considered they had a right to their share. They would have preferred to play their part on shore, and it was not their fault that they were constrained to stay on the ship, guarding prisoners who were more numerous than themselves. The storm blew up to such an extent that Anson found it necessary to intervene. In the morning he called all hands to the quarter-deck and made it clear that there would be an equal distribution amongst them. All the stuff was brought to the quarter-deck to be divided in proportion to each man's rank and commission. The Commodore added that he was throwing in his entire share for the men who had carried out the attack.

Walter says that this business was thus by the Commodore's prudence settled to everybody's satisfaction. This, however, was far from the truth. Repercussions from these arguments, and from the distribution of prize money when the voyage was over, were to end as causes before the Court of Admiralty and these contentions were to drag on for three years before final judgment was passed in May, 1747.

It took all that day to settle the controversy of the plunder. By nightfall they had still not sighted the *Gloucester* even though they searched the area she was patrolling. But the next morning at ten they saw and chased a ship which, when they came near enough at two in the afternoon, proved to be the *Gloucester* with a small vessel in tow. Captain Mitchell later reported to Anson that in all his cruise he had taken only two prizes. One was a small snow with a cargo of wine, brandy and olives in jars and about £7,000 in specie. The other was a large boat or launch which *Gloucester*'s barge captured near the shore. The prisoners on this craft, although pleading poverty, saying that all they had on board was cotton, were discovered eating pigeon pie from silver dishes! Some of the jars were opened and nothing was found in them but cotton. But when the cargo was removed into the *Gloucester* and examined more carefully, every jar was found to contain amongst the cotton a considerable quantity of doubloons and dollars amounting in all to some £12,000. This splendid hoard was on its way to Paita: it was part of the property of the merchants there who, having just lost one fortune, now lost a second. *Gloucester* had also attempted the capture of two or three other ships which had escaped—a major disappointment as one of them was reported to have a cargo of immense value. Augmented by *Gloucester* and her prize, the little fleet set off to the north to make either Cape St. Lucas, California, or Cape Corrientes on the coast of Mexico.

Anson's decision to sail northwards marked the end of his activities in the South Pacific. While still at Juan Fernandez, he had seriously considered the possibility of crossing the isthmus of Panama to join forces with Admiral Vernon's expedition in the Caribbean. Although Vernon's operations were strategically unrelated to his own, the journey—with the aid of Indian guides—was feasible and might enable him to get the reinforcements from Vernon that he sorely needed. It was even possible that the two forces could combine for an assault on Panama, the capital. This scheme was given up when he learned, from papers captured in the *Carmelo*, that Vernon had been defeated at Cartagena.

Accordingly Anson turned his thoughts to the chances of intercepting the Manilla galleon on her annual voyage. He knew that, as in past years, she must already be at sea and making for Acapulco. The timing seemed satisfactory. It was only the middle of November and the galleon could be expected to arrive at her destination in the middle of January. There was, however, a difficulty in this plan. Anson had not obtained enough water at Paita for his ships and he could not undertake a long voyage without replenishment. Provided that he could find supplies, and allowing four or five days for watering the fleet, he calculated that his Squadron should reach their station off Acapulco in a little over a month. Where to go for water was therefore his first problem. All he had to guide him were the accounts of former voyagers, supplemented by information obtained from his prisoners. From his experience of these early accounts Anson had become wary of putting any reliance on their statements.

Anson's voyage took place rather more than 200 years ago. Today, it is not easy to remember that practically nothing was known of this area of the world at the time when this particular voyage was made. The instruments of navigation available to mariners were still primitive and inadequate for their purpose. Positions quoted on charts bore little relation to fact, and errors of several degrees of longitude were constantly being discovered in the earlier guides. In the latitude of the equator an error in time of one minute would mean a distance of something like 15 miles. Before Harrison created his wonderful timekeepers such a discrepancy was much better than normal and 50, 100, or 150 miles were common errors in making landfalls. As the sand glass was the normal timekeeper at sea such inaccuracies are not surprising. The watches that no doubt travelled with the officers would have been no more reliable. The chronometer was able to keep accurate time to within one second per day.

It is of considerable interest to find that Harrison's first chronometer was taken on board the *Centurion* to Lisbon in 1736 on the recommendation of members of the Royal Society. It was not kept on *Centurion* but returned in the *Oxford* with a certificate of

*Harrison's No. 1*
*chronometer*

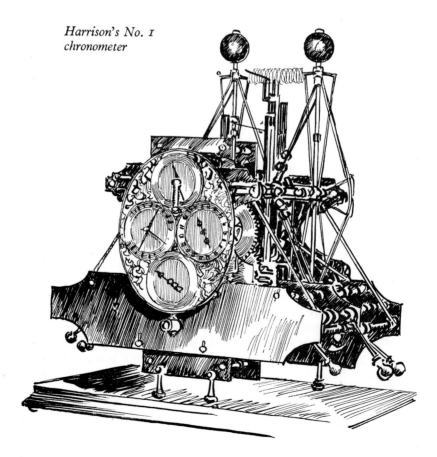

trustworthiness. The sextant had been invented by Sir Isaac Newton in 1699 but nothing had been done about it. It was rediscovered in 1730 but took somewhere near ten years to develop. So that the navigators in Anson's fleet were unlikely to have possessed the means of making any more accurate calculations than their predecessors.

For water, then, Anson decided to make for the island of Coiba near the isthmus of Panama. He had thought of Cocos Island which, whilst on a more direct line with Acapulco, was well out in the Pacific and nothing was known of its water potential. And the possibility of its not being found in the place ascribed to it on the available charts could have meant many days searching with no assurance of its discovery.

By now there were eight ships in the Squadron making it a sizeable force. A few days of sailing in company, however, showed that the *Solidad*, which had been reported to them as such a good ship, and the *Santa Teresa* were unable to keep up with the fleet and Anson accordingly ordered both to be cleared of everything of value and then burnt. Provisions, spare spars, sails, ammunition, rope, blocks and bosun's stores generally were transferred to the other ships. The value of these things to the Squadron, many thousands of miles from a friendly port, was considerable and the manning of the remaining ships became that much less of a problem.

Instructions were given to *Gloucester* and the other prizes and a rendezvous fixed. On 22nd November they came in sight of the island of Plata. One of the prizes was sent closer in to look for possible ships and for water which some accounts had reported there —accounts, which, if true, would save the journey to Coiba. But the prize found neither stream nor ships. Later in the day *Gloucester* sent off some of her prisoners in the Spanish launch to the mainland which was at this point only 7 miles off.

During this time the boats were kept busy distributing provisions through the fleet to ensure that each ship should have enough food on board for six months. The fact that after more than two years at sea they were still consuming some of their original intake of provisions gives some idea of the enormous load of foodstuffs with which the expedition had originally set out. It will be remembered that Anson had been worried by the congestion of bags and boxes on his gun decks, but undoubtedly this great stock had played no small part in their preservation.

The Manilla galleon was Anson's next objective. As he had heard from prisoners that one of these ships was of great size, he had eight swivel guns mounted in each of *Centurion*'s fore and main tops. When the Squadron crossed the equator they entered the belt of tropical rains and found that after so long a stay in the drier southern latitudes the seams of their topsides and decks required caulking to keep the ships dry. By 27th November, Captain Mitchell had cleared the largest prize of her provisions and useful materials and she was scuttled and set on fire. The fleet, now numbering five ships, all good sailers, kept well together. On 3rd December, they came to Coiba but had to wait until next morning before attempting to make harbour because of suspected shoals in the channel.

A point on the island was safely cleared by all the ships except *Gloucester* which had to tack and stand well to the southward. The others lost sight of her. Twenty-four hours of tacking back and forth finally carried the rest safely to their anchorage. The watering place was easily discovered and in two days they had laid in all the wood and water required.

One article of food with which they first became acquainted on Coiba was greatly appreciated after their enforced abstinence from fresh meat, broken only at rare intervals. This was turtle, which was easily caught and available in quantity. The crews thought it most delightful food and were at a loss to understand why the Spaniards would not eat it. They contrived to take a number of them to sea when they left the island and these proved a welcome and excellent addition to their basic rations. Oyster fishing was carried on at Coiba but the sailors when they tried to eat them found them unpalatable. These were pearl oysters, and Walter records that the

*Eight swivel guns in each of* Centurion's *fore and main tops*

Spaniards of Panama and the neighbouring coasts employed negro slaves to dive for them and says that formerly a great number of them were engaged in the industry. The negroes were carefully trained and were not considered to be fully competent until by degrees they had learned to stay under water at great depth for so long that they bled at nose, mouth and ears. Once that had happened they were able to dive with much more facility than previously and were neither worried nor subject to a further occurrence of the trouble. The same sort of work is still being done by Greek sponge divers who suffer in the same way.

In three days the Squadron was ready for sea, but was weather-bound in the anchorage by contrary winds. Once clear of the island, more time was wasted in a search for the missing *Gloucester*. On 10th December a sail was seen, raising their hopes, but she proved to be a bark from Panama, on her way to Cheripe. Eventually, on the 12th the *Gloucester* rejoined the fleet and Captain Mitchell reported that when they tacked to the southward on first coming to the island they had sprung their fore topmast which had kept them from working to windward and so regaining the Squadron. The last capture, the *Jesu Nazareno*, which had nothing on board of real value, was sunk and they stood to the west after nine days at Coiba, full of impatience to get to grips with the Manilla galleon.

# 12

# *Treasure Galleon*

THE COMMODORE now issued instructions to the commanders of all the vessels, naming the various rendezvous and courses to be adopted in the case of separation. Haste was urged in making the passage to the north of Acapulco where they were to close with the land and then work their way up the coast about 30 miles from the shore, until Cape Corrientes lay abreast of them.

Cruising in that area was to continue until 14th February on which date they should proceed to the middle island of Las Tres Marias, where if the Commodore had not turned up, the ships were to be wooded and watered and then to set a course for Macao. Anson's strategy was based on the expectation that they would have the trade wind and a good passage to Acapulco. For nearly a month, however, they had contrary winds and storms alternating with dead calms and heavy rains, and it was Christmas Day before they saw Cocos Island, estimating it to be about 300 miles from the mainland.

It was 9th January before they actually picked up the true trade wind which stayed with them steadily for the next eight days. After that they were not so fortunate. Nevertheless they progressed steadily and on 26th January having got far enough to the north they stood eastward towards the land and Acapulco. Anson calculated that two days' sailing should bring them within sight of the coast, but on the 28th although the weather was perfectly clear, there was no sight of land all day. They held on the same course after dark presuming that they would find their destination in the morning. At about ten o'clock that night a light was seen to port and *Tryal's Prize* from a mile ahead signalled that she had seen a sail, upon which, of course, everybody was certain of its being the long-hoped-for galleon. A light was being shown which doubtless must be the vessel signalling to a consort. So *Centurion* cast off the *Carmelo* which they had been towing and signalled *Gloucester* to join them in the chase. All hands were at stations and the strange light was followed for the whole of that night, sometimes appearing to be quite close and at others somewhat further off. There were those on board who swore they could see the vessel's sails and the Commodore himself was so sure of overhauling his quarry that he gave orders for the great guns to be loaded with double shot for the first broadside and after that with one ball and one grape.

Thus they carried on throughout the night in constant expectation of catching the enemy and laying hands on the enormous fortune buried in the hold of the fat galleon ahead. Imagine the universal disappointment and chagrin when as morning light broke no ship was to be seen and what they had been following so determinedly all night was a light on shore! A point of considerable interest to them was that when they first saw this light it could not have been less than 80 miles away and yet nobody on board had had any doubt whatever, throughout the 'pursuit', that it was anything but a ship's light. Later it was discovered to be a fire on a high mountain which glowed for several days. When the sun rose they found themselves about 25 to 30 miles from the shore.

Amongst the few prisoners still remaining on board were a Spanish pilot and two Indians, who were the only men on the ship who claimed to have been in this part of the world before. When two hills came into sight they declared them to be over the harbour of Acapulco. Although by the reckoning of Anson's officers these hills were in the wrong latitude, the three men stuck to their assertions. They also affirmed that the fire which had deluded everybody was in fact proof of the expected arrival of the galleon for such fires were lit as signals when the galleon was late in appearing. This information, being exactly what everybody wished to hear, lulled the English in believing what they might otherwise have questioned.

So they continued to cruise, not sure whether the galleon had arrived or not. It was already the middle of January and although the three natives assured them that the galleon sometimes did not arrive until the middle of February serious doubts began to arise in their minds. Anson needed a harbour to give his men a rest: he also wanted positive information of the galleon before deciding either to carry on with the search or to call it off and replenish the Squadron's stores. He questioned the prisoners very carefully and upon their answers resolved to send a boat at night into Acapulco harbour to see if the galleon was there or not. One of the Indians was positive that this could be done with absolute confidence and a minimum risk of discovery.

On 6th February the barge with two officers, a Spanish pilot and the Indian set off. After an absence of five days it returned, and the officers told Anson that no harbour had been discovered anywhere near the spot indicated by their two guides. The barge had therefore sailed eastward for about a hundred miles and found numerous sandy beaches but could not land on any of them because of the breakers. At the end of their run they could just make out in the distance two hills which they concluded must be those near Acapulco, but as they were running low in water and provisions they turned back to the *Centurion*. Anson straightaway made sail with his fleet towards this more likely spot and when they arrived within a reasonable distance of it on 12th February he dispatched the barge once again. The officers were to take the greatest precautions to avoid being seen from the shore. During the next day those in *Centurion* observed high land in the distance which they presumed was Acapulco. When after six days the barge had not returned, there were grave fears for her safety, but on 19th February she rejoined the fleet and Anson was informed that he was still about 150 miles from Acapulco!

*Three negroes tried to jump overboard*

It appeared that in the early hours of the morning of the 17th the barge arrived at an island at the mouth of a harbour. The Spanish pilot and the Indian who were taken with the party again had no idea of where they were. Whilst the crew rested on their oars a light was seen on the surface of the water a short distance off and with as little noise as possible they were able to surprise the occupants of a fishing canoe. In it were three negroes who immediately tried to jump overboard to swim the short distance to the beach, but when a musket was pointed at them they changed their minds and were taken into the barge, and the canoe was pushed adrift against a rock where it would no doubt get smashed up. This it was hoped would deceive anyone finding the bits into presuming the drowning of the negroes. Having taken this precaution the crew rowed out to sea as hard as they could and at dawn had the satisfaction of finding themselves far enough from land to discount the likelihood of being observed.

The three negroes were of supreme value to the Commodore who could now obtain the information about the galleon on which his future movements depended. It was with mixed feelings that he heard their story. Although the chance of intercepting the galleon before her arrival at Acapulco was lost, other conditions had arisen which might still change their luck. The galleon had made harbour some twenty days previously and had finished discharging her cargo. She was now taking in water and provisions for her return and the Viceroy of Mexico had issued a proclamation fixing her departure from Acapulco on the 3rd March. With this news everybody recovered their excited hopes of the treasure-laden ship at last falling into their hands. How much better it was going to be to capture her on her return when her chief cargo would be the cash she had just received in payment for the goods she had carried from Manilla. Things were looking up. They could almost feel the silver jingling in their pockets.

At this point in his narrative Walter inserts a chapter giving an account of the commerce between the city of Manilla on the island of Luconia (now Luzon) in the Philippines and the port of Acapulco on the coast of Mexico. Since the days of Elizabeth I every English seaman had heard of the fabled Spanish galleons packed with treasure, but few knew anything of the highly organised Pacific traffic which was Anson's objective. Walter was not a little proud of being able to give a description of it, especially as he had to translate from Spanish records.

He began his account by summarising the papal bull issued in 1493 by Pope Alexander VI. The voyages of Portuguese and Spanish navigators had opened the sea-routes to India and to the new world of the Americas: and there was an obvious danger of a clash between Portugal and Spain, the two strongest supporters of the Papacy. To avert this rivalry and to ensure the peaceful propagation of the Catholic faith, the Pope allocated all new discoveries west of a line drawn one hundred leagues west of the Azores to Spain: those east of the line went to Portugal. This demarcation was changed, by mutual agreement a few years later, to one of 370 leagues west of the Cape Verde Islands, the 50th degree of longitude west of Greenwich.

Needless to say, this arbitrary division of the new world did not please the other seafaring nations who were excluded, amongst them the English. 'But', says Walter sourly, 'it seems the infallibility of the Holy Father had, on this occasion, deserted him, and for want of being more conversant in geography, he had not foreseen that the Spaniards, by pushing their discoveries to the West, and the Portuguese to the East, might at last meet with each other, and be again embroiled; as it actually happened within a few years afterwards.' Magellan's circumnavigation of the globe and his passage of the straits named after him opened the Pacific to Spanish ships— 'proving', says Walter, 'the long disputed fact of the earth's spherical shape'. His voyage also enabled the Spaniards to lay claim to the Philippines as a possession of the Spanish Crown. The claim was of great importance to Spain in that the islands gave opportunity for trade with both China and the coveted East Indies, which lay within the Portuguese sphere.

Communications were quickly established between the Philippines and Peru. The city of Manilla, built on Luzon, the chief island of the Philippines, soon became the mart for all Indian and Chinese commodities which were each year carried across the Pacific for sale. In the Americas these goods were paid for in silver and this was the principal item of cargo on the return voyage. Manilla prospered. The Spanish Government quickly recognised the value of the business and in a series of edicts brought it under strict control.

In the early days the traffic was conducted between Manilla and Callao and on this trip the ships were continually favoured by the trade wind. Although the two places were between 9,000 and 12,000 miles apart the voyage was often finished in little more than two months. But the return journey was of a very different nature, sometimes taking over twelve months to complete. The reason for this was that at first the returning galleons stayed within the limits of the trade wind which, of course, meant battling against the breezes which were so helpful on the outward journey. It is said that a

Jesuit first suggested that the ships should clear to the north of the wind belt and thus benefit from the prevalent westerlies to California. This practice was adopted and continued for the next 160 years. At some time fairly early in this period, the American port for the trade was changed from Callao to Acapulco. It is recorded that in 1586, Sir Thomas Cavendish engaged a galleon off the southern tip of California which had come from Manilla, from which it can be assumed that the custom of sending the treasure vessels to Acapulco must already have been established by that date.

The island of Luzon was well situated for this Chinese trade, and the bay and port of Manilla were reckoned among the most remarkable in the world. The bay is a circular basin almost land-locked, nearly 30 miles across, and on its eastern side is the port and town of Manilla—large and populous. The port was named Cabite and lay about 6 miles to the southward of the town and here the ships engaged in the Acapulco trade were usually stationed. For these ships, the departure from Manilla was somewhat of a problem as the passage lay through channels between islands in which, says Walter, 'the Spaniards by reason of their unskilfulness in marine affairs, waste much time, and are often in great danger'.

The traffic carried from here to China and parts of India was principally in goods for the Mexican and Peruvian markets. These comprised spices and all sorts of Chinese silks and manufactures, particularly silk stockings of which no less than 50,000 pairs was the usual quantity on the annual ship. There were vast quantities of Indian stuffs—calicoes and chintz, much worn in America, and some small articles such as goldsmith's work made by Chinese in Manilla itself. All these goods were collected together at Manilla for the annual voyage to Acapulco. The town was said to contain 20,000 permanent Chinese residents either as servants, manufacturers or brokers.

*In Manilla*

The trade to Acapulco was not open to every merchant in Manilla but confined within particular regulations somewhat analogous to those by which the trade of the 'register' ships from Cadiz to the West Indies was governed. The galleons were found by the King of Spain who paid the officers and crew. Their tonnage was divided into a certain number of bales of standard size which were allocated amongst the convents at Manilla, principally to the Jesuits, as a donation for the support of their missions for the propagation of the Catholic faith. The convents had the right to ship the tonnage of goods on board in proportion to the number of bales they had been granted; or they could, if they so wished, sell the privilege of shipment to others. As the merchants who took these shares were often without stock it was usual for the convents to lend them considerable sums of money on bottomry. Royal edicts limited the value of the annual cargo. Walter says that some manuscripts which he had read gave the figure of 600,000 dollars. However, from many sources and calculations he was certain that the return could not be less than three millions of dollars.

When at the end of the round trip the galleon reached Manilla, the profits of the voyage were divided and distributed throughout the East, a fact which led the home-based merchants of Spain to complain that they were at a disadvantage in competition with their Eastern counterparts. Mexico and Peru were less dependent on Spain for their necessities than they thought desirable or politic and the silver which should, in their opinion, have come to Spain was going to the East. Apart from the Crown, the only people to benefit were the Jesuits on the other side of the world. Don José Patinho when Chief Minister of Spain, who disliked the Jesuits, attempted to loosen their control of the traffic by regulations forbidding the entry of Indian commodities into any Spanish port in the West Indies, except such as were carried in the 'register' ships from Europe. But the Order was powerful and its influence prevented strict adherence to the regulations.

The annual ship, or ships—for there were occasionally two—sailed from Manilla during July and arrived at Acapulco in December, January or February and, having landed their cargo, started the return journey in March planning to reach Manilla in June. The round voyage thus took a year. There was always a second ship ready to sail when the first returned and for this reason the trade was provided with three or four stout ships, to ensure that in case of accident the business did not come to a stop. The largest of these ships, the name of which Walter could not discover, can have been little less in size than an English first rate, because in one cruise against the English East Indiamen she carried at least 1,200 men.

The other vessels, though smaller, were fifty-gun ships and carried from 350 to 600 people, passengers included.   As these were King's ships, commissioned and paid by him, the senior Captain was styled the General and carried the Royal Standard of Spain at the main topgallant masthead.

When the ship had all her cargo aboard and was ready for sea, she weighed from the mole of Cabite about the middle of July, and taking advantage of the westerly monsoon proceeded to sea.   When 30°N had been reached they reckoned to get the westerlies which would carry them bravely all the way to California.   Walter possessed copies of a manuscript chart which had been taken from one of the ships, showing the track of the vessel both out and home.   Marked on the chart were all the known discoveries and as no port had been found between the Philippines and the coast of California, the anchor was not let go until arrival at Acapulco, a journey of some six months. The most astonishing thing about such an extremely long cruise at that time was the Spaniards' ability to get fresh water; and Walter, knowing that these ships carried many passengers, was keenly interested to find out how it was procured.

He learned that the Spanish seamen in the South Seas carried and preserved their water, not in wooden casks as the English did, but in earthenware jars which were very like the large oil-jars seen at that time in Europe.   When the Manilla ship first put to sea, more water was taken on board than could be stowed between decks and the jars containing it were hung all about the shrouds and stays so that from a distance the ship looked very strange.   Although it was not possible to carry a six months' supply in this fashion, and though the manner of procuring further supplies might seem uncertain, the galleon made the long journey without trouble.   That such large numbers of people were willing to risk a terrible death on such a lengthy voyage suggests that the ships rarely came to grief through water shortage.   The extra water came from the clouds— the rains encountered between the parallels of 30°N and 40°N—and a most ingenious method of collecting it had been developed.   A great number of mats were taken to sea and when the time came these were placed sloping against the gunwale in one continuous line. The lower edges of these mats rested in the trough of a split bamboo which served as a gutter and all the water falling on the mats was thus collected and drained off into jars.   So successful was this way of adding to their supplies that, notwithstanding the accidental manner of the delivery, it had never been known to fail and it was not uncommon for all their water jars to be filled several times over.

If they managed such long voyages without dying of thirst, there were other dangers to beset them which occasionally took their toll.

8

The worst of these was scurvy brought about by the inordinate length of the voyage without fresh vegetables and, as Anson had found, the cause of the death of a great number of men. The galleons, of course, carried very rich cargoes and therefore the captains were inclined to be unnecessarily cautious in the handling of their command. It was said that they never set the mainsail and often lay hove-to all night. The sailing instructions for the captains appeared to have been drawn up by someone more scared of a gale—even a favourable one—than of the terrible consequences of a long and tedious voyage. The orders were that captains should make their passage in the latitude of 30° as far as possible and no further northward than absolutely necessary for getting a westerly wind, whereas the English masters considered that further north the winds were much brisker and steadier, and to them the whole management of these voyages by the Spaniards was far from efficient. By setting a course in latitudes 40°N to 45°N the English considered the journey might be accomplished in half the time, but the ships would have to take their share of rough seas and gales.

The Manilla galleon maintained her easterly course to the longitude of 96° where they generally found a plant floating on the sea which they called *porra*.*

This was the point at which the galleon turned southwards. So important was the sighting of this weed to the voyagers that the whole ship's company would customarily chant a solemn Te Deum in thanksgiving for their safe crossing. Keeping the *porra* well in view they coasted southwards without attempting to close the land until they were on a line with southern California. Cape St. Lucas was their first point of contact both to confirm their position and to find what enemies, if any, were in the area. Attention was specifically drawn to this point in the captain's instructions.

The reason for this was that the Jesuits maintained what amounted to a coastguard and look-out station at Cape St. Lucas. Here the natives were trained in agriculture and viniculture, and a good stock of wine, fruit and water was held locally for the voyagers. The captain was therefore ordered upon sight of the signal fires on shore to send his launch with a guard of twenty well-armed men and the year's letters from the convents at Manilla to the Californian missionaries. This boat was to bring back the provisions which would have been prepared and also any news of possible enemies lurking in wait for them. If the coast was clear, the captain proceeded to Cape St. Lucas, then to Cape Corrientes, from which he

---

* *Puerro* is Spanish for leek. *Porra* is a word which whilst generally used in a tropical sense is sufficiently near to *Puerro* to have been used in Anson's time to serve the same meaning. *Porreta* signifies the green leaf of onions or garlic.

went on to Acapulco. The galleon usually reached port in the middle of January, but navigation was so uncertain it could be a month earlier or later.

Acapulco was the finest and most secure port in all that part of the Pacific coast. The harbour was a basin surrounded by high mountains, but the town was reckoned a wretchedly unhealthy place and was almost deserted for nine months of the year. The mountains prevented the circulation of air and the only fresh water had to be brought from a considerable distance.

Whilst in port, the galleon was moored to two trees on the west side of the harbour, the cargo being unloaded with the utmost dispatch. The town suddenly came to life. As soon as the news spread that 'the ship had come home' merchants flocked in from all parts of Mexico to lay in the stocks of luxury goods required by their business for the coming year. Payment was made in silver. This was shipped, together with a small quantity of goods destined for Manilla, such as cochineal, articles of millinery from Europe and sacramental wine—all being articles that required little space. Fresh provisions and water were taken on board as soon as the sale of the ship's cargo was completed. Speed in fitting out the galleon for sea was essential as the captain was under orders to start the westward journey before 1st April.

*The galleon moored to trees*

In marked contrast to the bulky cargo carried on the journey from Manilla, the homeward cargo consisted mainly of bullion. Because of this great dissimilarity the ship was equipped in different fashion for the respective voyages. When the galleon left Manilla for Mexico it was deep laden and the lower tiers of guns was struck into the hold until such time as the vessel approached Cape St. Lucas and might expect enemies: and only just sufficient hands to work the ship were carried in order that fewer provisions were required to be stowed. But the return trip was—or ought to be, says Walter—made with all her guns in place. The crew was strengthened with additional sailors and one or two companies of foot to reinforce the garrison at Manilla. Many merchants taking passage also, the total personnel on the return was little short of 600 who were amply provisioned owing to the space available for stores.

The return journey was made in latitude 13°N or 14°N until Guam in the Ladrones was reached, where by royal instructions fires were lit every night during the month of June for the ship's guidance. A small garrison was maintained on the island for the express purpose of attending the galleon and its requirements. As the mooring was not good the ships rarely stayed more than a day or two but sailed off as soon as water and other necessaries were on board. The next place of call was Cape Espiritu Santo on Gamal where the captain was again ordered to look out for signals. Sentinels were posted not only there, but also in Catanduanes, Butuzan, and the island of Baton in the Philippines. These look-outs were to make a fire as soon as the ship was sighted and the captain took notice that, if the blaze was extinguished and then four times relit, he was to understand that there were hostile ships about. The shore station would tell him what and where this menace was, and he would take whatever action seemed best, not forgetting to advise Manilla of his whereabouts. If after the first fire there were only two relightings, he could assume that all was well, Such, in summary, is Walter's account of this remarkable Pacific traffic.

# 13

# Too Late

THE MANILLA galleon was due to sail on the 3rd March. This vital piece of information had been supplied by the three negro fishermen, but they were able to give other news which was also of great interest to Anson. The attack and sacking of Paita had been reported to the Governor of Acapulco who at once set about strengthening the defences of his own town. A guard was placed on the island at the harbour mouth and had been withdrawn only forty-eight hours before the arrival of *Centurion*'s barge. Had the barge not been delayed in locating the town she would undoubtedly have sailed into the fire of the enemy and either been sunk or seized, with the loss of her entire crew.

The fact that the Governor had withdrawn his guard pleased Anson as it suggested that the Spaniards could not have seen the barge and were not expecting an attack in the near future. The barge had returned on 19th February so that the Commodore decided to stay on his station and wait for the galleon to the westward of Acapulco where there was little likelihood of being seen from the shore—the one hazard which, it was thought, could upset his plans. To turn the time of waiting to good use the men were employed in scrubbing the ships' bottoms, and in adjusting the trim of the vessels. Orders, signals and stations were laid down and rehearsed in readiness for the attack on the galleon when she put to sea on the 3rd, the day fixed by the Viceroy for her departure according to the negro prisoners.

On the 1st of the month they drew close enough to see the high hills usually called the paps, over Acapulco, and took up the stations laid down in the Commodore's instructions. The ships were ranged in a semicircle with a radius of 45 miles from the town. Each ship was 9 miles from the next and therefore the *Carmelo* and the *Carmin* at the ends of the arc were 36 miles apart. The approach of any vessel could be seen at a distance of 18 miles from each end so that the whole sweep within which no ship could pass unseen was just on 72 miles. By means of their signals every unit in the line could be speedily informed of anything seen in any other section of it. To make as certain as possible that no ship should slip through their net, the *Centurion*'s and *Gloucester*'s cutters were to lie all day 12 to 15 miles from Acapulco, and to shorten the distance at night. Should the galleon be seen, one of the cutters was to return to the Squadron and let Anson know which direction it had taken, whilst the other was to follow the enemy at a distance and direct the fleet by means of lights.

The prisoners had given a flattering account of the size and armament of the expected galleon and during their vigil the Squadron made ready to meet her to their best advantage. Anson presumed that only the *Gloucester* and *Centurion* were capable of lying alongside her and so *Centurion* took on board all hands from *Carmelo* and *Carmin* except such as were necessary to handle those vessels. And from *Tryal's Prize* ten Englishmen and as many negroes were sent to supplement *Gloucester*'s company. The serious lack of men was to some extent mitigated by the use of negroes, of whom there were a fair number on board, and to them Anson promised freedom if they would play their part in the coming action. For two months past these recruits had been training at the great guns and were now quite able to serve them and, as they had been fairly treated by the Commodore, they seemed well pleased to help.

On 3rd March, every man was keyed up in anticipation of the galleon's departure from Acapulco, but all that day and the following night passed without sight or news of it. Though vexed and disappointed they did not give up hope that some delay had been occasioned by the merchants and that the ship would come out. So they persisted with a good look-out. The 7th March was Sunday, the beginning of Passion week, which they knew the Papists observed strictly by abstaining from all forms of labour: the galleon could not, therefore, be expected before the next week. On the Friday of Passion week, the cutters returned and gave it as their considered opinion that the galleon could not possibly have left without being sighted by them. On the 15th the cutters went back to their station and hopes ran high until, with no news of their quarry by the end of that week, the majority realised that their presence must have been discovered and that the galleon would not sail that season. And this, as they later learned, was in fact what had happened—the barge had been spotted when looking for the port of Acapulco.

Anson whilst saying nothing had secretly concluded that they had been observed and so, as an alternative operation, formed a plan for taking Acapulco. After weighing up all the methods and studying such plans as he possessed and comparing possible methods of assault, he decided upon a surprise attack by night as the plan likely to give the best chance of success. But inquiring of the natives about the local conditions which might affect the scheme he was told that the winds upon which he would be dependent were certain to be adverse and that any idea of setting out to arrive in the night could be discounted. With this difficulty and the thought that even yet the galleon might sail—for he was not absolutely certain that his Squadron had been discovered—he decided to keep station a while longer. The length of his stay would, of course, be governed by their stores of provisions, wood and water and also by the date on which they must leave for China. The cutters were ordered to remain at their posts until 23rd March.

Anson called the fleet together and made a signal to speak with all the commanders in order to review with them the stocks of fresh water remaining in the fleet. Investigation showed that it was imperative to obtain fresh supplies immediately, and they decided that the harbour of Sequataneo or Chequetan, now called Zihuatanejo, which was the nearest to them, offered the best chances. They thought also that the galleon might even yet try to slip to sea, and to counter that possibility *Centurion*'s cutter, under command of Mr. Hughes, the Lieutenant of the *Tryal's Prize*, was ordered to cruise off Acapulco for twenty-four days.

The Squadron set off to the westward, but calms and adverse currents slowed their passage to a considerable extent. During the calms Anson set the crews to clearing the *Carmelo* and the *Carmin* of the most valuable part of their cargoes for he intended to destroy these two ships as soon as possible.

By 1st April they had by estimation come near to Sequataneo and two boats were sent off to range along the coast for the best watering place. The boats were gone some days and the Squadron's casks were becoming alarmingly short of water. However, a number of turtle were caught which were very welcome in view of the fact that they were once again on salt provisions, which in the hot climate was almost unbearable. The only sources of information on water supplies were the writings of buccaneers and with only a few days' supply left it was not difficult to foresee calamity. But the boats

*The Spanish method of obtaining water*

turned up on 5th April with the news of water in a place called by Dampier Chequetan and were sent back by Anson the next day to sound the entrance and the harbour. On the 7th, they again returned to report all well, and the fleet made for the harbour. *Centurion* and *Gloucester* entered at the same time but the *Carmelo* and *Carmin* had to be brought in by the *Tryal's Prize* as they had dropped far astern. It was two days before these three joined the Commodore.

So after four months at sea, since leaving Coiba, and with only six days' water left between them, the Squadron once more came to land to replenish and refit. The water flowed from a brackish lake, but at the spring head, half a mile inland, it was fresh and soft. Of necessity, in spite of the extra transport involved, this pure water had to be used and so Anson arranged for several canoes to work a shuttle service of small casks from the spring to the beach. Here they were emptied into larger casks to be taken aboard the ships.

The country round about was well peopled and cultivated so that they had hopes of a quick and satisfactory provisioning. To effect this Anson sent forty well-armed men on a march inland to start an exchange of goods, for which he proposed to use the trade goods which had been brought on board at Portsmouth. The men were instructed to act circumspectly and offer no force or hostility, but they returned the same evening so exhausted that some had to be carried.

They estimated they had travelled 10 miles on a road that was clearly in common use by horses or mules. About 2 miles from the harbour the road forked into the mountains, and they took the eastern branch but met with no villages or people. The officers put up poles with notices in Spanish suggesting that the inhabitants come to the harbour and do business with the Squadron, but not a soul appeared during the whole of their stay at the place. Had the party proceeded along the western fork they would have come across a village within 2 miles.

Anson sent Lieutenant Brett with a boat party to examine the harbour of Petaplan and report on its possibilities as a watering place. When the crew numbering sixteen landed a number of armed horsemen appeared who, it seemed, were ready to drive the English off but as soon as Brett ordered his men to fire, the horsemen made off, quite obviously anxious to avoid a conflict. There were about 200 of them. Accordingly a boat was stationed to watch this stretch of coast to ensure that the cutter which was cruising off Acapulco should not run into trouble on its return.

As the local inhabitants of Chequetan could not be found and no trade could be commenced, Anson refrained from any further attempt to contact them and set about collecting whatever provisions were available in the immediate locality.   Fish there were in plenty and besides such well-known types as bream, mullet, sole and lobsters they also caught cavallies, fiddle fish and sea eggs, and also the 'Torpedo or numbing fish which as a flat fish much resembled the thornback'.   Walter tried the experiment of touching one to achieve the numbness of which he had heard.   The effort produced the promised result and he successfully deadened his arm.   Turtle were still procurable from the boat stationed at Petaplan and although they had been eating it for six months it was still appreciated by the crews being, indeed, the only fresh eating they had during the whole time.   In fact the fruits and anti-scorbutic plants were neither palatable nor abundant and the turtle provided most of their diet.

They decided that Chequetan left a lot to be desired as a haven for mariners.   Yet it was ideally suited for watering, wooding and, most important, as a jumping-off place for an attack on the Manilla galleon.

Whilst all the work ashore was going on, Anson was occupied with the problem of his future operations.   His manpower situation was serious.   Once again, they were about to enter areas where storms could be expected, and the total number of men available in the Squadron was insufficient to man and fight a fourth-rate warship. The *Carmelo* and *Carmin* were unloaded as far as it was possible to make use of their cargoes, although not more than a tenth of the total was taken out.   After consulting with his commanders he resolved to destroy the *Tryal's Prize* as well.   This excellent ship was in good repair but the need to man her depleted the crews of the *Centurion* and the *Gloucester* to such an extent that in really bad

*Walter tests the numbing fish*

weather all three ships might be in jeopardy. All the usables on
board *Tryal's Prize* were therefore removed into the two men-o'-
war and *Carmelo, Carmin* and *Tryal's Prize* prepared for scuttling
with the greatest possible despatch.

On 1st April, 1742, the officers of the *Tryal's Prize* wrote a petition
to Anson praying him to forbear destroying the prizes which would
put officers and men out of pay. On 14th April Anson replied in
a letter to Captain Saunders of the *Tryal's Prize* explaining how it
had become necessary in view of the manpower situation to reduce
the Squadron to *Centurion* and *Gloucester*. By this means these two
ships would be better manned and much more fitted to contend with
the monsoon weather in the China Seas. Saunders was instructed
to discharge all his people into *Centurion* and *Gloucester*. Officers
and servants, petty officers, seamen and marines were to become part
of the complement of the two ships.

Owing to the laborious manner of transporting water on board and
the time taken to carry out essential repairs to the rigging and a
multitude of smaller refitting operations, it was the end of April before the Squadron was in condition to leave. One incident of some
importance occurred during their stay. Near to the spring-head
where they filled their water casks there ran a well-trodden path into
the interior. It was the only such path and to safeguard themselves
from any attack by the Spaniards they cleared a space by felling trees
some little way inland and kept a constant guard on the barricade.
At the first alarm, all the men employed at the spring—there were
forty working on the casks—were to march instantly to this post.
Although primarily intended to prevent sudden attack, yet this place
answered the other purpose of preventing the sailors from straggling
into the country and being captured by the Spaniards. Should such
a capture have been made by the enemy they would have no doubt
gained a knowledge of Anson's circumstances and future designs
that would, of course, have been very welcome to them.

*The cook stripped by the Indians*

The sentinels were under the strictest orders to let no one pass and yet, despite these precautions, one man disappeared. He was a Frenchman—the Commodore's cook—and it was at once assumed that Papist sympathies had led him to desert and betray the expedition.    Long afterwards it was discovered that he had been captured by Indians who took him prisoner to Acapulco, from where he was sent to Mexico and then to Vera Cruz, being later shipped to Spain. He managed to escape ashore at Lisbon where the British Consul gave him asylum and sent him to England where he brought the first news to reach the authorities at home of the course and fortunes of the Squadron.    Lewis Leger, for that was his name, told his story of how, being turned back by the sentries at the barricade with threats of punishment, he had then gone off to find some limes for Anson's table.    In the woods he was surprised by four Indians, who stripped him and took him naked to Acapulco.    He suffered severe treatment at every stage of his captivity and the Spaniards lost no opportunity of venting upon him the hatred they had for anybody caught interfering in their possessions in the Americas.

This poor man, having survived the hazards of Anson's voyage and of captivity in enemy hands, was killed a few weeks after his arrival in London, in a miserable street brawl.

Although the Squadron never was attacked at Chequetan, they saw the smoke of fires in a semicircle around their position and just before they left the place these fires increased in a manner that suggested considerable reinforcement in preparation for an attack. On 27th April the three doomed ships were beached and their upperworks filled with combustibles.    The next morning *Centurion* and *Gloucester* were warped out of the harbour in a light air and then one of the boats went back to set fire to the three ships.    A canoe was left moored to a grapnel in the middle of the harbour.    In it was a message in a well-corked bottle, to Mr. Hughes, who had all this time been keeping his watch on Acapulco.

Anson was certain that his presence at Chequetan must by now have been reported to Acapulco and he believed that, as Chequetan was right off the course that the galleon would take, she might after all accept the risk and put to sea.    Hughes in *Centurion*'s cutter it will be remembered was instructed to cruise off Acapulco for twenty-four days and then to go to Chequetan.    There was a strong likelihood of his missing Anson when he returned and so the letter in the bottle directed him to return to Acapulco where he would find the *Centurion*.    Anson wrote that he would cruise for him there for a number of days, after which the Commodore would go south to join the rest of his Squadron.    This last sentence was inserted for the benefit of Spanish readers if they found the canoe (which they did),

but it would not deceive Hughes who knew that Anson had neither a
Squadron to join nor any intension of returning to Peru.

The stormy season was approaching and they were anxious to get
on their way to China.   There was nothing left for them to do on the
American coast where they had delayed long enough, but they must
first look for Hughes and his party.   The cutter was already a fortnight overdue and Anson could only suppose that she, her six hands
and the Lieutenant had been captured: but this was no certainty, and
the two ships stood towards Acapulco to search for her.   *Gloucester*
kept inshore of *Centurion* and at night they hove-to and showed
lights.

When the strain of waiting for their companions, who were the best
of picked men, became too much, the Commodore under the firm
impression that the boat must indeed have fallen into Spanish hands
decided to send a letter to the Governor of Acapulco.   In this Anson
said that he would release all his prisoners if the Governor for his
part would return the cutter's crew.   There were several Spaniards
of some consequence among the prisoners who, it was thought, might
sway the Governor's decision and so a Spanish Officer whose honour
they trusted was picked to take the message.   He was provided with
a launch and a crew of six other prisoners who all gave parole for
their return.   All the rest of the prisoners had signed a petition
asking the Governor to do what was proposed in Anson's letter.

*The missing cutter*

The Commodore was now in high hopes that the next twenty-four hours would bring an answer as they were staying close to land, but the next day the ships were blown out to sea. Fortunately the gale subsided quickly and all sail was made to get back to Acapulco and in a short time the mast-head look-out called to the deck that he could see a boat approaching under sail far off to the south-east. They soon made it out to be the missing cutter which they at first assumed had been sent off by the Governor, but when the boat reached them the appearance of the crew showed them to have suffered hardships far in excess of what could have been put on them even in a Spanish prison. The men had to be helped on board and were immediately put to bed, where rest and food from the Captain's table brought about their recovery.

Hughes reported that, when their appointed vigil off Acapulco was up, he had started westwards to join the Squadron, but in spite of all their exertions the cutter was swept back down the coast. Shortage of water soon compelled a search for a place ashore to replenish their stock, but everywhere they found the surf too great for landing and in an extremity of thirst they were reduced to sucking the blood of turtles which they caught. Just when they had given up hope, they were saved by a heavy rain which they caught in spread sails and filled their casks. With renewed life they stood to the west with a strong current aiding them and fifty hours later were picked up by the Commodore. They had been at sea in an open 22-foot boat on a dangerous coast for forty-three days.

There was nothing at all now to detain Anson as he needed no answer from the Governor. Except for some negroes and mulattos, he gave all his prisoners their freedom. Fifty-seven in all were put into two launches with masts, sails and oars, together with provisions and water for fourteen days. Thomas says that 'the boats left about four in the evening after having, although they were enemies, observed "the custom of seafaring people at parting by wishing us a prosperous voyage"'. These boats, it was learned later, arrived safely.

*Centurion* and *Gloucester* stood immediately to the south-west in order to pick up the trade winds which by all accounts were much brisker and steadier in that direction. On 6th May they saw the last of the mountains of Mexico, well content that in a few weeks they would arrive in the Canton river, meet many English ships, talk with fresh people and enjoy some civilised living after twenty months entirely cut off from all contact with their own kind.

# 14

# *Failure and Sickness*

A LL THE accounts which Anson had read indicated that the trade winds should be found about 200 miles or so from land on the parallel of 13° or 14°N. That was the area where the Pacific was usually crossed in a westerly direction. *Centurion* and *Gloucester* soon reached the correct latitude and by their reckoning were well over the prescribed 200 miles from the coast. To their dismay, however, the wind blew in their faces or else hardly blew at all. They tried every trick to find the trades, but it was seven weeks—time enough to have reached Asia—before they got the true trade wind and even then they were not yet a quarter of the way across!

The outlook for Anson and his men grew rapidly worse. All the hardships they had endured when rounding the Horn and in the South Pacific a year before returned in force. Both ships were in a state that called for a dockyard refit and soon after leaving Acapulco they found a spring in *Centurion*'s foremast. This was a crack which went about 26 inches round the mast and about 4 inches deep. The carpenters had no sooner fished this than the *Gloucester* was in trouble with a bad spring in her mainmast 12 feet below the trestle trees. The mast was so rotten that the sole remedy was to cut it down to the spring which left a stump unfit to carry sail and useful only to step the topmast. Further time was lost in making these repairs—and time was the one thing they could not afford.

Scurvy had reappeared.   There had not been a single case of it since they left Juan Fernandez.   Their previous experience made it plain that only a speedy passage would now save the remaining force from serious loss of life, and the chances of this in their condition seemed hopeless.   In the middle of June, 1742, Thomas recorded 'the abundance of scorbutic symptoms' and towards the end of July he wrote: 'About this time our people began to die very fast, and I believe above five parts out of six of the ship's company were ill and expected to follow in a short time'.   Some believed that the warmer climate might lessen the effects of the disease and that the previous outbreak was caused by the severity of the weather in the high southern latitudes at the Horn, but they were soon disillusioned.

Walter gives an account of the efforts made to halt the progress of the trouble, and through all his remarks runs a tone of gentle surprise that nothing they did was successful.   He was quite certain that fresh provisions, plenty of water and fresh air were of great importance even if they did not prevent or cure.   From his own findings it was clear to him that once the thing got a hold, the only means of allaying it was to get the victims ashore or, he says, bring them into the neighbourhood of land.   He wrote one paragraph which is worth recording:

Perhaps a distinct and adequate knowledge of the source of this disease may never be discovered: but in general, there is no difficulty in conceiving that as a continued supply of fresh air is necessary to all animal life, and as this air is so particular a fluid, that without losing its elasticity, or any of its obvious properties, it may be rendered unfit for this purpose, by the mixing with it some very subtle and otherwise imperceptible effluvia: it may be conceived, I say, that the steams arising from the ocean may have a tendency to render the air they are spread through, less properly adapted to the support of terrestrial animals, unless these steams are corrected by effluvia of another kind, and which perhaps the land alone can supply.

At the foot of the page in my copy is a note in pencil:

Effectual Remedies have been since discovered consisting of substances which contain fixed Air, such as Malt and other preserved vegetables.

The *Centurion*'s surgeon had ascribed the death roll during the passage round the Horn to the shocking weather which had been experienced.   He now did his best to cope with this new epidemic, but at last admitted defeat, declaring his complete inability to prevent or cure the illness.   At this Anson himself took a hand and decided to try the effect of two medicines which were apparently being

9

much vaunted when the expedition left England. These were 'the pill and the drop of Mr. Ward'. Walter says here that it was now kill or cure. One man swallowed his pill. After a violent nose-bleed he slowly recovered and although having previously been at the point of death he managed to survive. One is inclined to think that the British tar could stand anything and that in this instance the recovery was in spite of the pill. Some others received a little bene-fit but in general the disease marched on unhindered.

The two ships struggled along with their sadly weakened masts and sickly crews and at last picked up the trade wind. It was not very strong and *Centurion* could have carried all her sails. But *Gloucester* had become a travesty of a ship with a stump mast. She sailed so poorly that *Centurion* was forced to set only topsails in order to stay with her and was continually hove-to in order that *Gloucester* could come up. These delays accounted for a loss of at least a month on this passage.

After nearly four weeks of the trade wind the ships had reached a point some 300 miles from the Ladrones. On 26th July the wind came westerly and held them up for four days and then fell away completely, leaving the ships rolling heavily in a swell. This proved too much for *Gloucester* and her fore cap split under the strain. Down came the topmast and in falling smashed the foreyard at the slings. *Gloucester* was now so badly crippled that she was unable to make any sail until repairs had been effected and there was nothing for it but that *Centurion* must take her in tow. Twenty men were sent from the Commodore's ship to help with the work and were away for eight to ten days.

The repairs to the spars were just finished when a heavy storm drove from the west compelling them to heave-to. Under this blow *Centurion* sprung a leak of such a size that everyone, officers included,

Gloucester *was a wreck*

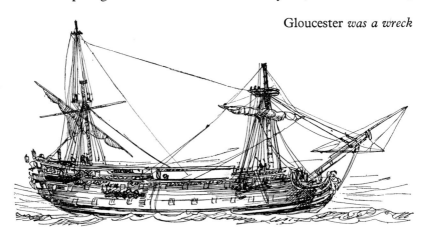

was needed for continuous toil at the pumps to keep the influx of water under control. Then *Gloucester*'s newly repaired topmast came down again, followed very soon after by her main topmast which was doubled to the stump of her main-mast. Anson knew that his consort was now in dire trouble. Without *Centurion*'s assistance she could do nothing and *Centurion* was unable to assist, for a large number of the crew were down with scurvy while the remainder, all the able-bodied men, were required to man the pumps.

When the gale abated and the two ships could come together once again Captain Mitchell reported a further disaster. In addition to the loss of her masts overboard, *Gloucester* had sprung a leak, and her officers and men were pumping for their lives. There was 7 feet of water in the hold even though they had been at it for twenty-four hours. Captain Mitchell begged for the assistance which he so desperately needed, but Anson was utterly unable to do anything for him beyond sending a boat to discover the full extent of the damage. *Gloucester* was a dying ship. Her stern-post was loose and working at every roll: two beams amidships had broken in the orlop which the carpenters declared could not be repaired at sea. Continuous pumping had so exhausted the men that they could no longer maintain their efforts, even with the water gaining on them. Their casks and provisions were under water and the ship was in such a crazy condition that everything was loose and the quarter-deck ready to collapse. Out of ninety-seven people on board only twenty-seven were capable of any work on the ship and several of those were gravely weakened by illness.

Anson immediately sent provisions and water, but it was obvious that even if *Centurion* could spare men to aid *Gloucester*, which was not possible, their combined efforts could not keep *Gloucester* afloat. The only course was to transfer her crew and remove as much as possible of her useful stores before she was destroyed. The weather had improved and the Commodore sent as many men as he could spare to Captain Mitchell's assistance. The work of clearing the ill-fated ship took two days and fortunately the weather stayed calm. Anson had a great need of two cables and an anchor but owing to *Gloucester*'s heavy rolling and the physical weakness of the men, it was impossible to manoeuvre the tremendous weights involved. With considerable difficulty they transhipped the prize money into *Centurion* but the prize goods were abandoned, and these were worth several thousand pounds. All that could be saved of the provisions were five casks of flour, three of which were spoiled by sea water. The seventy sick men of the crew were placed in the boats as carefully as possible but nevertheless three or four of them died as they were being hoisted into *Centurion*.

By 15th August everything possible had been removed from *Gloucester* and her hold was full of water, yet the carpenters thought she might float for some time if the weather stayed calm.   Anson knew that they were somewhere near Guam and that their enemies would be glad to get hold of even the wreck of such a ship, so she was set on fire.   The wind being still light, there was some risk of damage from blast if she blew up too soon, but although she burnt fiercely all night the explosion, when it did come at six in the morning, found them 12 miles away.   The explosion was a small one but the *Gloucester*'s end was marked by a huge pillar of black smoke which shot up to a great height.

The general hope was that *Centurion* would now complete her voyage without any further setback.   With *Gloucester*'s crew aboard there would be additional men for handling the ship and, after their long spell of misfortune, it seemed reasonable to think that their luck had turned.   But the storm which had finally settled *Gloucester*'s account had driven them northward of their intended route and *Centurion* was found to be not in latitude 13°N as was thought, but in 17°N.   They had no idea whether the ship had reached the longitude of the Ladrones.   As I have mentioned earlier, the navigators of the time were severely handicapped in their reckoning by the lack of any sure method of determining longitude.   Anson's problem could have been solved at once by a chronometer.   Many years were to pass before this instrument formed a part of the standard equipment issued to the Navy and even as late as 1815 it was unusual for British men-o'-war to be supplied with chronometers, except when on convoy duty.

The calm continued for four days.   Anson was acutely anxious in case they had passed to leeward of the Ladrones without knowing. If this were so, then they could not expect to see land until they reached the eastern part of Asia, some 1,000 or 1,500 miles away. By that time scurvy would have decimated his crew.   Moreover, they would reach Asia at the height of the monsoon when only a strong ship and an equally strong crew could hope to make a port. The deaths from scurvy began to increase rapidly—eight, ten and sometimes twelve a day being buried, while the men who had so far managed to keep clear of the disease were beginning to show the familiar symptoms.   The carpenters were set to locating the leak, which, although the weather was still calm, had increased considerably.   They discovered it in the gunners' fore store-room.   The water was rushing in under the breast hook on either side of the stem, a place in which it would be impossible to effect a repair before they arrived in port when it could be got at from outside.   The carpenters did what they could from inside which did reduce the flow of water somewhat, to the great relief of everybody, although it no wise completely stopped the trouble.

When at last the calm broke, the wind came from the south-west, entirely contrary to what was required. On 22nd August a current was setting them southwards and on the 23rd at daybreak two islands appeared to the west about 45 miles away, at which their excitement and urge to close the land rose to feverpoint. But the wind fell away. Another twenty-four hours found them drifted farther westwards and in sight of a third island, close enough to send off a boat to look for an anchorage. When it returned with the report that there was no place for a ship to anchor, and no hope of provisions, their newly recovered spirits flagged again. After this disappointment a gale drove them southwards, and it was obvious to all on board that if they did not quickly find another island where they could get ashore, their days were numbered.

Gloucester *blows up*

# 15

# Timely Haven

ON 27th August, 1742, they sighted a group of three more islands, 30 to 40 miles to the eastward. Course was immediately set for the middle one, but the winds fell away and the following day found them still 15 miles off. The alarm was given when a proa appeared between the islands of Tinian and Aquiquan —as they later learned them to be named. The fact that the Spaniards always kept soldiers at Guam made it necessary for Anson to prevent them from recognising his ship. In her present condition *Centurion* could not fight and it was imperative that the enemy should not discover their terrible weakness. So he mustered all hands capable of standing to arms; loaded the upper and quarter-deck guns with grape-shot, and to allay suspicion showed Spanish colours, hoisting a red flag at the fore topmast head to give *Centurion* the appearance of the Manilla galleon and to encourage the locals to come aboard. In this disguise they closed the island at three in the afternoon and sent the cutter ashore to find a place for the ship.

The ruse was successful for a proa came away to meet what was assumed to be the Manilla galleon. The cutter picked up the proa and took it in tow to the *Centurion* and a pinnace was sent to relieve the cutter so that the latter might proceed with her task of finding a haven. On board the proa were a Spaniard and four Indians and the Spaniard was immediately pressed for information about the produce and conditions on the island. To his heart-felt relief Anson learnt that it was uninhabited and contained everything that he could wish for in the way of food—fruits, flesh, fowl and water in abundance. The Spaniard told him that the garrison at Guam used the island as a supply store and that he himself was a sergeant sent here with twenty-two Indians to jerk beef which he would load on board a 15-ton bark then lying at anchor near the shore.

His account was soon verified. As the *Centurion* approached the shore, herds of cattle could be seen grazing in pleasant surroundings and the island had all the appearances of a splendid plantation with woods and lawns of a lovely quality. A lucky accident when all seemed lost had by contrary winds driven them to a place most fitted for the recovery of the sick, the repair of the ship and replenishment of their stores.

It was essential to prevent the rest of the Indians from escaping in the bark mentioned by the Spaniard, to give news of Anson's arrival and so the pinnace was sent off to capture it. In a short time *Centurion* let go her anchor. The weather was calm and in normal circumstances there should have been no difficulty with the operation, but the physical condition of the men still able to work was so poor that it took five hours to furl the sails—a job that would normally be done in as many minutes. In fact the total number of hands— *including* those absent in the pinnace and cutter—able to stand-to and handle the ship was seventy-one! These were all that remained of the combined crews of *Centurion*, *Gloucester* and *Tryal*, which when they left England had numbered nearly a thousand.

When the sails were furled the rest of the night was given over to sleep. They were whacked, and rest they must have. In the morning an armed party went ashore to capture the landing place and to overawe the Indians should they prove hostile. But these had run off to the woods when they saw the bark seized. There were a number of huts which saved the sailors the bother of erecting tents. One hut, 50 by 40 feet, was straightaway cleared for use as a hospital and as soon as it was ready the sick men—128 of them— were taken ashore. As at Juan Fernandez, Anson and his officers shared in the work of carrying those who were too weak to help themselves.

The advantages of living ashore were demonstrated once again, for the men began to make a rapid recovery. And here it is interesting to note that Walter records that the benefit from acid fruit was most noticeable and that its use put most of the sick on their feet in a week. Twenty-one men died in the first two days but only ten more succumbed during the rest of their two months' stay. The place was dry and healthy, pleasant to look at and stocked in luxuriant fashion. At first they shot the cattle they required for meat but this was a waste of powder and the men learned to capture them quite easily—as easily as the poultry which abounded in the island. Wild hogs were a different matter. The ferocity of these creatures necessitated shooting them or running them down with large dogs which Indians in the past had trained to the work. The dogs followed the sailors without any trouble but most of them were killed by the hogs. During the whole of their stay no ship's bread was eaten, the seamen much preferring the breadfruit which was discovered there. From Walter's description there can be no doubt that for two months the crew lived like fighting cocks—the best of everything and as much of it as they could tuck away. The recital of various animals, birds, fruits, vegetables which they obtained so easily reads like a menu of Christmas fare.

Naturally, the men wondered why there were no people living in this paradise. The island, it appears, was used as a larder for others in the neighbourhood and on inquiry Anson learnt from the Indians the story of its depopulation. For this island of Tinian, in company with Rota and Guam, was once full of people, Tinian alone having at least 30,000 inhabitants. Fifty years previously, however, an epidemic had raged amongst the islands destroying many thousands.

*The leak at the stem*

To make up their diminished numbers the Spaniards evacuated the remaining people of Tinian to Guam, but, as is the way of a people taken from their homes and freedom, most of them died of grief within a few years. To dispel any doubts about the figures of the population, Walter goes on to say that pyramidal columns, architectural features and ruins were to be found in great numbers everywhere. The Indians assured him that these columns which were 5 feet square at the base and 13 feet high, with an inverted hemispherical cap, were the foundations of buildings and that these buildings were dedicated to a certain religion. The pillars were arranged at 6-foot intervals in two rows, 12 feet apart, and the enormous quantity of them demonstrated very plainly the size of the original population.

Only one fault was to be found at Tinian and that was with the anchorage. It appears that the bottom was sharp coral rock which if the weather turned rough could play old Harry with their cables. The monsoon, now blowing, was likely to cause trouble when the moon changed. Apart from the risk from monsoon winds there was a tide race between Tinian and a small island called Aquiquan which raised a great overfall and backwash so that boats in the area were in great danger of being pooped.

All hands who could be spared were accordingly employed in arming the cable with a good rounding several fathoms long from the anchor, which meant winding a mass of old rope about the cable as a protection against chafing. Then they turned their attention to the leak by the *Centurion*'s stem. It was necessary to raise the bows of the ship out of the water. On 1st September they began to shift the guns aft to settle her by the stern so that the carpenters could get at the trouble from the outside. They ripped off the sheathing and caulked the seams on both sides of the cut-water, afterwards covering them with lead and fixing new sheathing on the bows down to the waterline. When they hauled the guns back into place, the water began to squirt through the cracks as badly as ever so that they were compelled to start the job afresh. This time they emptied the fore peak of 130 barrels of powder and raised the bows higher than before. Once more the carpenters ripped off sheathing, recaulked and resheathed, and to their dismay found that as the guns were moved forward the leak burst open again. It was now evident that they could do no more than patch up inside and put in some more caulking. This stopped the leak for a time, but when all the guns were in position and the stores were re-stowed, the water again forced its way through. They let it be, knowing full well that the stem itself was at fault and nothing could be done until they could heave the ship down.

Anson himself went down with scurvy.   A special tent was erected for him on shore, as in their experience recovery was expedited by living on land for a spell.   Those hands who were well enough to do duty returned to the ship and began to prepare to get fresh water aboard.   So far the coopers had been too ill to fit up the casks.   The anchors were weighed and the cable examined for chafe from the coral rocks below.   Anson ordered the section of the cables next the anchors to be armed with chains and extra rope reinforcement, and the fore and main yards were lowered to help the ship should the expected violent gales occur.

By 18th September, at the new moon, they were prepared to meet whatever wind might blow, though in fact for the next three days all was well.   On the 22nd a violent gale from the south blew their confidence to ribbons.   The position was desperate.   The greater part of the crew was ashore, including Anson himself, and it was out of the question to attempt to get a boat to the ship.   The cables could not hold indefinitely and at five in the afternoon the small bower parted, leaving the *Centurion* swinging to the best bower. Tide set against wind and a large tumbling swell broke all around them.   The long-boat astern was suddenly thrown so high that it smashed the rails of the Captain's gallery and nearly killed the boat

*The long-boat smashes the stern gallery*

keeper. At eleven o'clock the best bower gave way. The sheet anchor which was all they had left was immediately let go, but before it reached bottom they were driven from 22 into 35 fathoms. They veered away a whole cable (600 feet) and two-thirds of another and, when they took a cast with the lead and found ground at 60 fathoms, it was obvious the anchor was on the edge of a bank and would not hold long.

Saumarez, who was the senior officer on board, ordered guns to be fired and lights shown as a signal of distress to Anson, but this served no purpose and a short while after a sudden squall drove the ship out to sea.

Anson with many officers and the greater part of the crew, amounting in all to 113 men, were left on the island. Those on board *Centurion* were far too small a party to handle the ship in weather of the sort they were experiencing while those on shore were marooned and unable to help in any way. The odds were that they would never see the *Centurion* again.

*Practising with muskets*

# PART FOUR
# Reward

# 16

# Rogue Ship

THE NOISE of the storm completely cut off the report of Saumarez's guns from those on shore, while the frequent lightning overpowered the flash of the discharges. When daylight came, *Centurion* had disappeared. Some of the men thought her lost for certain, and others that she would never be able to work her way back to the island even if she had not sunk.

They were 600 miles from the nearest port, which was Callao, and the only boat available was the little bark of 15 tons captured on their arrival at Tinian. This small craft was incapable of carrying more than a quarter of the party, and it was highly improbable that a European ship would ever come to the island, if indeed any other than *Centurion* ever had. In due course the Governor of Guam was sure to hear of their presence. Imprisonment was an unpleasant certainty but the Governor might equally well decide to treat them as pirates and order their execution.

Outwardly Anson remained unperturbed by this predicament. Plainly, his first duty must be to hearten his men and, after consulting his officers, he mustered all hands for a talk. He began by explaining that the chances were that *Centurion* had survived. As sailors, he thought they would know that she was well able to endure punishment and that if she did not return in a few days, as hoped, then the conclusion must be that she had driven so far to leeward of the island that she could not get back but would have to stand on for China. From this it followed that they must devise some way of getting to China themselves and rejoining *Centurion* there. The method he proposed was to haul the Spanish bark ashore and to cut her in half and lengthen her by 12 feet, which would bring her to near 40 tons, large enough to take most, if not all, aboard. He had, he said, spoken to the carpenters who agreed that the scheme was feasible if every man did his best. Anson would do his share with the rest and would expect no more from any man than he could perform himself. He stressed the urgency and the necessity of getting to work at once, on the assumption that *Centurion* would not be able to put back—which, indeed, was his secret opinion.

His address was well received, but, although it succeeded in putting fresh heart into the men, their response to it was at first disappointing. The majority preferred to wait, believing that *Centurion* would return and save them from the labour of lengthening the bark. It was not until some days had gone by with no sign of the ship that they were ready to get down to work. Once fairly started they worked with a will, to Anson's great relief.

About this time two boats appeared heading for the island, which everyone thought could be none other than *Centurion's* survivors. She must have gone down. Anson was so overcome that he had to take himself to his tent until his emotions were under control. A little later, when the two craft proved to be proas, he became anxious lest his men's presence should be discovered and ordered them to take cover in the undergrowth in readiness to capture the Indians if they landed. The proas, however, stopped a quarter of a mile offshore and remained motionless for nearly two hours before standing away to the south.

Under the circumstances the lengthening of the bark was a tremendous undertaking. Had they possessed a dock and all the tools and materials, it would have been well within their power as a naval crew but, lacking many necessities they had to improvise. The reconstruction of the hull was only one part, even if a big one, of Anson's problems. The bark, when the hull was completed, would have to be rigged and victualled for a voyage of 2,000 miles to China and safety; and, as the work proceeded, several unforeseen hitches arose any one of which might have brought Anson's plans to a halt.

Fortunately the carpenters of both *Gloucester* and *Tryal* with their chests of tools were ashore when the ship was blown to sea. The smith was also ashore with his forge and some tools but without his bellows: and a pair had to be improvised before he could begin work. There was no prepared leather to hand but they had hides and lime and soon produced a leather that was perfectly satisfactory for the job although it stank horribly. A gun barrel did duty for the pipe.

Trees were cut down and converted into plank. This proved to be a most laborious job and Anson took his turn at sawing. There were not enough blocks and tackle to haul the bark up the beach so they contrived to get it ashore by means of rollers and for these the smooth trunks of coconut palms were just the thing. Little labour was required to fit them for the job. Holes were made in the ends for hand spikes. A dry dock was dug and ways laid for the ship to be drawn up. Whilst all this was going on, a party was busy killing cattle and preparing provisions for stocking the bark when she was ready.

One good circumstance had a considerable bearing on the work and the speed with which it went forward. There was no hard liquor ashore. The only alternative to water was coconut milk which was a welcome and cooling drink.

The problem of rigging proved fairly simple. The bark's own sails and tackle was supplemented by the tents and spare cordage which had been landed from *Centurion*. They had plenty of tallow and lime to pay the ship's bottom and in general they felt happy about her equipment, but they were far from content about her size. Only half of the crew could possibly find room below deck and should it be a case of all hands there was no question but that the ship would overturn, because they were unable to improve her burden to 40 tons.

The food situation was equally difficult. There was no grain or bread of any kind. As a substitute the men ate breadfruit, which would not keep at sea. Although there were plenty of cattle they had no salt to cure beef for the voyage. They found some sun-dried or 'jerked' beef, the property of the Spaniards, on the island when they arrived but the quantity was too small for the number of men and the distance to be sailed. Anson decided to rely chiefly on coconuts, to use the jerked beef as sparingly as possible and in place of bread to use rice which could be obtained from the island of Rota where, he was informed, the Spaniards had large plantations worked by Indians.

Rice was therefore essential. To get it, however, would mean the use of force and this, in turn, raised further problems. On survey-ing his resources Anson was dismayed to find that he only had enough ammunition and powder for ninety charges for the firelocks—less than one shot apiece for the entire crew. With this meagre store he had to be content, but plainly nothing could be spared from it for the slaughter of cattle. With the details of the vessel and her equipment settled, and the work going ahead, Anson was free to con-sider the course to be steered; and this brought to light another problem which even his ingenuity and perseverance could not solve. There was neither compass nor quadrant on the island. Anson had, indeed, brought a pocket compass on shore for his own use but Brett had borrowed it to do a little surveying among the islands and he was now on the *Centurion*. Eventually, by great good luck a sailor found a compass in a chest in the bark. It was little better than a child's toy but it was invaluable. Then a few days later a quadrant was found on the beach and Anson's immediate problem seemed to be eased.

Fourteen days after *Centurion*'s unpremeditated departure they pulled the bark on shore and in the course of two days she was carefully sawn asunder. The iron-work was well in hand and the timbers and planks for the lengthening, even if rough in workmanship, were sawn and ready. The two halves were set the correct distance apart and on 9th October the task of joining them was put in hand. By now the entire ship's company was fired with enthusiasm for the venture and so well did the work proceed that it became possible to fix the approximate time of completion and launching. Anson estimated that they could put to sea on 5th November.

On 11th October one of *Gloucester*'s men, from a hill in the middle of the island, saw the *Centurion* on the distance and lost no time in letting those on the shore know. Anson, for the first time in the knowledge of his companions, lost his self-control and throwing down his axe rushed with the rest to the beach in a frenzy of excitement. When the ship was near enough, a boat was sent off with eighteen men to aid the crew and take them fresh meat and fruit. The next day the *Centurion* after nineteen days of frightening absence came to anchor once again.

Naturally those on shore could barely wait to hear the story. During the violent gale of 22nd September two cables had broken and from a third hung the only remaining anchor, which had pulled adrift. The *Centurion*, after her anchors had failed, was in no state to ride out the storm but drove helplessly to leeward. There was not a gun on board lashed in place, the ports were not barred and the shrouds were loose. The topmasts were unrigged, and the fore and main yards had been lowered so that it was impossible to set any sail except the mizen to bring the ship under control. To meet this crisis Saumarez had only 108 hands, a quarter of the normal complement of a sixty-gun ship, and this number was composed of either boys or invalids just recovering from scurvy and in poor physical shape. Several of the men were negroes or Indians recently enlisted who could hardly be expected to be first-class material in such an emergency.

The violence of the storm soon had the ship taking in great quantities of water through the leak at the stem, the loose port lids and the scuppers. There was sufficient work at the pumps to occupy the

10

*Lengthening the little Spanish bark*

entire crew, but Saumarez was obliged to accept the risk of flooding and detail a party of his strongest men in a desperate attempt to get sail on the ship.   They were drifting towards the island of Aquiquan a bare 6 miles away and unless they brought *Centurion* under control very smartly shipwreck seemed certain.   Every effort was made to raise the main and fore yards in an endeavour to get some sail up and to weather the island, but after struggling for three hours the jeers broke and the men, by this time completely worn out, could do no more.   After a night of waiting for the shock of striking the shore, they were amazed at daybreak to find the island a great distance off. Miraculously the storm had driven the ship to the safety of the open sea.

Three days passed before the gale began to abate and they made another attempt to raise the yards.   The fore was got up and, as the main was being lifted, the jeers broke again and a man was killed at which work was given up for the rest of the day.   The next, 26th September, was one of ceaseless, back-breaking labour for all on board.   Officers and men struggled to raise the anchor which still dangled on the end of two cables beneath the ship.   It had to be raised or they could never approach the land through shallow waters without it biting.   Moreover, it was the only anchor they possessed and it had to be preserved.   After twelve hours at work they had the anchor in sight but with night falling they desisted and slept.   On the following morning the work was finished and the anchor once more hung at the bows.

Five days after being torn so violently from their anchorage they were at last able to sail instead of drift.   Saumarez set course for Tinian.   He estimated the distance at about 150 miles which he expected to cover in three days, but on 1st October there was no sign of the island.   On the 2nd they did, indeed, sight an island which was soon identified as Guam—not a welcome landfall as it held the Spanish garrison.   But Saumarez could at last establish his position and realised that the currents had set them about 130 miles westwards of his calculations.   Ten weary days of tacking followed in which every man had to lend his weight each time the ship went about—so feeble had his crew become.   On 12th October the ship at last dropped anchor at Tinian.

Now that *Centurion* had returned, Anson's first concern was to complete the watering of the ship.   He took up his quarters on board with all his chief officers and a good many of the men.   The loss of the long-boat, which during the gale had smashed to pieces against *Centurion*'s stern, made getting the water on board difficult. The casks were too large to transport in small boats and rafts were built for the work, one or two of which were lost in the tide rip.

Only three days after the ship's return a sudden gust of wind lifted their anchor, forced them off the bank and drove them to sea once again. This time seventy men who had been employed at the watering and provisioning were left behind. The two cutters were on shore, but these could not bring off the whole crew so the eighteen-oared barge was sent to the aid of the cutters, and a signal made for all who could to embark. The cutters came off crowded with men, but forty fellows who were at work killing cattle and hauling them to the landing place were marooned. The barge was left for them but the ship was soon beyond reach and they had to stay ashore.

*Centurion* was in better case than on her last rogue trip for on this occasion she carried off more men and the weather was good. Nevertheless it was five days before she managed to return to Tinian to the very great relief of those left behind who, indeed, despaired of seeing her again to the extent that they once more set about fitting the bark for sea.

Anson resumed the interrupted task of watering. Two sailors lost their lives at the well where, according to Thomas, the sides caved in and buried them. Millechamp gave a rather different explanation. 'John Cross and Thomas Sevens made too free with the commodore's bounty, grew Pott Valliant and Quarrelled and Fought on the Brink of a Well they were filling Water at, where lay a long Range of Casks on a kind of Diclivity supported only by that which lay nighest the Well, in their struggling they happening to move that Cask which with the weight of above twenty others that were behind it, forced them both into the Well and Rowled in after them, by which means they were both Drowned.'

By 20th October they had 50 tons of water on board which was considered sufficient for the voyage to Macao. Next day one man from each mess was sent ashore to gather as large a quantity of oranges, onions, coconuts and other fruits as could be picked for use of the messes at sea. When these supplies were shipped, the bark and the proa were burned, the boats were hoisted in and the *Centurion* weighed anchor, steering for the south end of the island of Formosa.

# 17

# Chinese Tricks

THE RUN to Macao occasioned Anson few worries. At a rate of some 150 miles a day friendly winds took them steadily towards their goal although rotten rigging and the perpetual leak kept all hands well occupied. The crew were now in good health and performed their duties cheerfully.

One point remained to be settled. They would certainly be obliged to come to anchor frequently when they made China, but the *Centurion*'s sheet anchor was too big for coastal work while not really heavy enough for bad-weather duty. Apart from these there were some small anchors, stowed in the hold, which had been captured from prizes, but these were too light for the *Centurion*. Eventually it was decided to fix two of the large prize anchors into one stock and to lash to 4-pounder guns between the shanks; and this combination made an adequate substitute for the lost best bower. A similar affair was put together for duty as a small bower so that once again the ship carried two sufficient, if unorthodox, anchors at the bows.

By the first week of November they were off Formosa where at night they observed a great number of fires which were thought to be signals for them to land, but, being anxious to reach Macao, Anson ignored them. On the 6th they sighted the mainland of China about 23 miles distant. They hove-to until morning and when the sun rose were amazed to find themselves surrounded by an enormous number of fishing boats. Walter estimated that there could not be less than 6,000 of them, most having five men aboard and none with less than three. As the *Centurion* continued westwards along the coast, they encountered other equally large fleets on their way.

Anson thought that it would be easy to obtain a pilot from amongst all these people.  Plenty of the fishermen came close to the ship and an attempt to persuade some on board by throwing a dollar piece was tried but unsuccessfully.  Language was the stumbling block, or so Walter believed.  It was only possible to communicate by signs and these were not understood.  The men tried the word 'Macao' which only resulted in the Chinese holding fish up to them —they afterwards found that the Chinese word for fish had a similar sound.  One thing that surprised the English was that the fishermen displayed no curiosity whatever in the *Centurion*.  It was presumed that such a ship had never been in those seas before and that there must certainly be some fishermen who had never seen a European ship at all.  Walter was very disturbed at this lack of interest by maritime people towards a strange vessel.  He noted this strange behaviour of the Chinese in other circumstances and put it down to 'a mean and contemptible disposition'.

Millechamp, no doubt soured by later experience in Macao, had a low opinion of the Chinese as mariners for, says he, 'they are wretched sailors and perform their little voyages at great expense'. He thought them ingenious, artful and treacherous and capable of

*Unorthodox anchor*

any crime to gratify their covetousness: so much for contemporary opinion of the inscrutable Chinese.

Being unable to learn anything from the fishermen as to the best course for Macao, Anson was forced to rely on his own judgment which, in the event, served well enough. All the way along the coast the fishing vessels continued to surround them and at last they managed to persuade one fisherman to direct them to an anchorage for the night. In the morning a Chinese pilot boarded them and in poor Portuguese intimated that he would take them to Macao for thirty dollars. This was paid at once and they weighed anchor and set sail. Soon afterwards several other pilots came on board producing certificates of competence from satisfied captains, and offered their services. Anson, however, stuck to the man already with him. He learned that they were now but a short distance from the port and that in Canton river there were eleven European ships of which four were English. The *Centurion*'s passage up the river was slow. Adverse winds obliged them to anchor so frequently that it was 13th November when they arrived off Macao.

Thus, after over two years of extreme hardship they found themselves once more in a civilised country and a friendly harbour— everything to make life tolerable and pleasant: all the requirements for the ship and possibly letters from home, and best of all meeting their own countrymen once again.

At the time of Anson's arrival, Macao was a Portuguese settlement falling into decay and existing by sufferance of the Chinese. Once it had been very rich and populous—well able to defend itself against the nearby Chinese Governors. In 1580 Portugal came under Spanish domination and during the next sixty years the Dutch seized Ceylon and the Portuguese territories in the East Indies with the result that, when Portugal again won independence, Macao was stripped of much of its trade and all its prestige, the 'face' to which the Chinese attached such high importance. In Anson's time the Portuguese were at the mercy of the Chinese authorities who could enforce obedience by the simple expedient of cutting off supplies from the foreigners and who tolerated their continuance because Macao was the only port frequented by European ships. In fact the Canton river provided a better harbour for them than Macao itself.

*Macao*

Here Anson found a problem. The Chinese were not used to entertaining European men-o'-war, far less to granting them the customary privileges, and he was worried lest he might inadvertently embroil the East India Company with the Regency of Canton by insisting on being treated differently from merchantmen. On consideration he nevertheless decided to go to the Portuguese Macao rather than the Chinese port of Canton.

Millechamp says that when *Centurion*'s crew arrived at Macao the Chinese threw stones at them in the street and called Anson the Grand Ladrone Captain; i.e. the great captain of the thieves. Anson knew how to deal with such insults and to command respect. As soon as he arrived he sent an officer with his compliments to the Portuguese Governor requesting that his Excellency advise him, by the same officer, as to his wisest course of action to avoid offending the Chinese. For it so happened that the four English ships lying in Canton harbour were John Company vessels and as these were virtually in the power of the Chinese, any offence on Anson's part might seriously affect them.

The Chinese authorities insisted that all ships using the port paid dues according to their tonnage. As men-o'-war were exempted from paying dues in all foreign ports, Anson most certainly was not going to derogate the honour of his country by paying anything here. The boat returned from Macao in the evening with two officers sent by the Governor. It was his opinion that if Anson ventured into Canton harbour, duty would assuredly be demanded, and so, if the Commodore approved, he would send a pilot to take *Centurion* into a safe anchorage at Typa—an island close to Macao belonging to the Portuguese—where she could be careened. This operation had become one of some urgency, but it was highly improbable that duty would be demanded if the ship lay at this place whilst careening.

This suited Anson very well and the following morning a Portuguese pilot steered them towards Typa. Beyond sticking them on the mud he did the job well enough. They kedged themselves off on the next tide and on arrival saluted the castle of Macao with eleven guns, and received an equal number in return. The following day, the 15th, Anson paid an official call on the Governor, being saluted on landing with eleven guns, which were returned by *Centurion*. The visit was not a mere formality, for Anson asked him for supplies of provisions and ship's stores for the *Centurion*. The Governor appeared anxious to help, but he made it clear to Anson that he dared not comply. It was out of the question for him to let them have anything at all without the Commodore first obtaining an order for it from the Viceroy of Canton. The Chinese, said the

Governor, supplied him on a day-to-day basis and they compelled his submission to any terms they chose to demand just by the threat to cut off supplies to Macao.   Anson was told that the proper person for him to apply to for his provisions was the Chuntuck—the highest civil officer in the two provinces of Kwangtung and Kwangsi.

Accordingly he decided to go to the Viceroy for a licence and for the purpose hired a Chinese boat for himself and his attendants. As he was about to step aboard, the Hoppo, or Chinese Custom House Officer at Macao, refused a permit to the boat and ordered the waterman not to proceed or else!   Anson tried his best with the Hoppo, as did the Governor, but all to no purpose.   So the next day, his temper no doubt slighty frayed, he told the Hoppo that if the permit were still refused he would man and arm his own boats for the journey—and did the Hoppo know anybody who would dare to oppose him ?   The Chinese were never that foolish.   The permit was granted, and Anson went to Canton.

On arrival he discussed with the officers and supercargoes of the English East India ships, as to what should be his best course of action for obtaining the licence.   He was advised to proceed in the fashion they pursued themselves and that was to go to work through the mediation of the principal Chinese merchants and not to approach the Supreme Magistrate direct.

In 1720 the Emperor of China first gave licences to certain Chinese merchants allowing them to trade with the 'Fankwae' or foreign devils on condition that they went security for their good behaviour and proper payment of customs dues.   The merchants formed themselves into a corporate body called the Co-Hong and built factories or merchant houses which stood in a line facing the river

*The Hoppo refuses a permit*

opposite Honan island. In front of them was an open square usually filled with a crowd of pedlars of fruit or sweets and craftsmen plying their trades. The factories were rented by the various East India companies from Hong merchants.

The English officers promised to use their influence with the Chinese merchants who, in their turn, undertook to submit Anson's application. A month passed productive of many excuses and repeated avowals of the near-completion of the business. At the end of it the Chinese blandly admitted that they had not, and dared not, apply to the Viceroy himself for he was too great a man. Having explained this to the Commodore, they then made plain to the East India officers at Canton that any meddling with Anson's affairs on their part would most likely create a lot of trouble for them with the Government. In the face of this the Company men could do nothing for Anson and quietly backed out of the affair.

Anson, seeing that no good would come of the intervention by the Chinese merchants, told them that he would proceed to Batavia and refit there, but that this was impossible unless he was supplied with sufficient provisions for the journey. The merchants immediately promised to let him have what he required, explaining at the same time that the business must be carried out secretly. The bread, flour and other foodstuffs would be put on the English ships which were now about to sail and these would stop at the mouth of the Typa where the *Centurion*'s boats could then receive them. The merchants let it be seen that they were doing the Commodore a great favour (for which they would no doubt expect a fair payment) and on 16th December he returned to the ship from Canton with the apparent intention of proceeding to Batavia as soon as the provisions were delivered.

In fact, he had no intention of going to Batavia. When he returned to his ship, he found the mainmast sprung in two places and the leak worse than ever. Even with provisions aboard he could not contemplate putting to sea without refitting, as the ship would most certainly founder, and he determined to have *Centurion* hove down before he left Macao. He had come to the conclusion that his recent course of action, taken on the advice of East India Company officers and intended to safeguard the Company's trade, had been the cause of his difficulties. Had he in the first place gone direct to the Mandarins who were the chief officers of State he would most likely have had everything granted and been able to leave in short time.

So he wrote to the Viceroy stating that as Commander of a Squadron of H.M. Ships of War, and having a leak in his ship and being in great need of provisions it was impossible for him to proceed till the ship was repaired and victualled.   He went on that, as a stranger to the country, he was unacquainted with the customs of the country and ignorant of the steps he should take to procure audience and therefore had to apply as he was now doing.   Anson finished by requesting His Excellency to authorise him to employ carpenters on the repair of his ship and to purchase provisions so that he could continue his voyage to Britain with the monsoon.   If he were delayed, he added, he might not be able to leave before the next winter.

This letter was translated into Chinese, and Anson delivered it personally to the Hoppo of the Customs and requested him to send it immediately to the Viceroy.   The Hoppo took it much as he might have handled a hot brick, giving so many excuses for not touching it, that Anson became suspicious of his collusion with the merchants who had continually objected to his having any contact with the Viceroy or Mandarins.   So the Commodore took his letter back, informing the Hoppo that he would have one of his own officers take it to Canton in his own boat under explicit orders not to return without an answer from the Viceroy.   The Hoppo, frightened at the possible consequences of his refusal, now begged to be allowed to deliver it and to procure an answer as soon as possible.

This he did, for the letter, written on 17th December, brought a reply by the 19th.   A Mandarin of the first rank with two others of lesser importance and a regiment of servants in eighteen highly decorated row barges, and with musicians and men, came to the *Centurion*.   A request was made for *Centurion*'s boat to escort the

visitor on board.   In his honour a hundred men of the crew were
drawn up under arms, in the uniform of the Marines.   The high
panjandrum was saluted with drums and what music they could find,
and he was met by Anson on the quarter-deck and conducted to the
great cabin below.   The Mandarin then stated that his business was
to check all the statements in the letter concerning the condition of
the ship and especially of the leak, for which purpose he had brought
two Chinese carpenters.   He had everything written on a paper
with a vacant space for his comments.   Walter states that this
Mandarin was a man of considerable parts, frank and honest to a
degree not usually found in the Chinese.   The two carpenters
reported the leak to be as bad as described in the letter and that
*Centurion* could not therefore proceed to sea without refitting.   The
Mandarin was satisfied with Anson's statements and asked to look
over the ship.   The size of the guns on the lower deck and the weight
and size of the shot impressed him tremendously.

   The opportunity was too good to miss.   Anson carefully explained
to him and his officers that a supply of green vegetables, so important to the health of his men, had been summarily suspended by
the Custom House officers at Macao.   He was sure that his guests
could see that he was well able to get what he wanted by force
although friendly people did not act in that way, but on the other
hand such people would not let friendly visitors starve and sink
in their harbours.   It was hardly likely, he went on, that his crew
would be content to starve, however, within sight of such plenty as
they could see around them: and then—and one detects the twinkle
in the Commodore's eye—if they should be reduced to cannibalism,
it would be the plump and well-fed Chinese who would become
food for his men.   The Mandarin told the Commodore that the
whole affair should be straightened out and he himself would
authorise the delivery of provisions regularly every day.

*A mandarin comes to*
Centurion

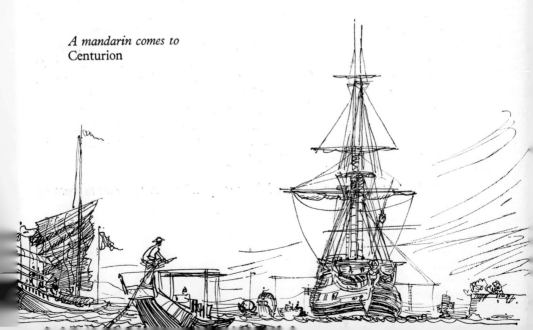

Anson then invited the three mandarins to dinner, and Walter notes their embarrassment with knives and forks and how one of the attendants had to cut their meat into small pieces for them. But he says that though they had difficulty with their eating, at drinking they were expert and accomplished. The Commodore excused himself from this part of the entertainment with a pretence of illness.

During the stay at Macao several people left the *Centurion*. Millechamp says that the officers who had been taken from the *Gloucester* and the *Tryal's Prize* now applied for leave to return to England, but Anson made it clear that shortage of men excluded the possibility of such a concession. He said also that Anson took care to send home Captains Saunders and Mitchell and Colonel Cracherode who, had they stayed, would of necessity shared any prize money that might come the way of *Centurion*.

Anson wrote in a letter to Saumarez on the *Centurion* on 30th November, 1742, '. . . I have used all the power I had with the commanders of the India ships to exchange such of the *Gloucester*'s and *Tryal's* officers as have an inclination to go home (for able seamen), but they put me off with excuses'.

Captain Saunders returned to England on board a Swedish ship and he carried despatches from Anson. In December soon afterwards Captain Mitchell, Colonel Cracherode, and Mr. Tassel, one of the agents' victuallers, with his nephew Mr. Charles Harriot returned on East India ships and says Walter, 'I, having obtained the Commodore's leave to return home, embarked with them'.

At Macao Anson heard for the first time of the *Severn* and the *Pearl*, which had last been seen off Cape Noir a year earlier, and of their safe arrival at Rio de Janeiro (Appendix III). He had given up both these ships as lost, more especially the *Severn* which he knew had much sickness among her crew.

Several days went by before Anson heard from the Mandarin. The *Centurion*'s presence had, it was said, provoked a crisis of diplomatic protocol. The French now chose to represent their Indiamen, some of which were anchored in Canton, to be men-o'-war. Their officers were jealous of the English receiving treatment in accordance with their standing as King's ships, while their own status remained merely that of trading vessels. Be that as it may, Anson's suggestion of his readiness to right himself by his own power if necessary soon had the authorities jumping to please him. His warrant for supplies came quickly to hand while Chinese carpenters and smiths were sent to begin repairs. Walter wrote:

And next day a number of Chinese smiths and carpenters went on board to agree for all the work by the great.  They demanded at first to the amount of a thousand pounds sterling for the necessary repairs of the ship, the boats, and the masts.  This the Commodore seemed to think an unreasonable sum and endeavoured to persuade them to work by the day; but that proposal they would not harken to; so it was at last agreed that the carpenters should have to the amount of about six hundred pounds for their work and the smiths should be paid for their ironwork by weight allowing them at the rate of three pounds a hundred nearly for the small work and forty-six shillings for the large.

Anson then set himself to getting the ship hove down to examine her bottom.  Two junks were hired from the Chinese—one to heave down by and the other to store the powder and ammunition whilst the operation was performed.  On a neighbouring island the ground was levelled and a large tent erected for storing the timber and provisions: and a hundred Chinese caulkers worked on *Centurion*'s weary seams.  All the preparations for careening and preparing the necessary gear took up a great deal of time—the caulkers were not rapid workers—and it was 26th January before the junks arrived. Materials purchased in Canton were a long while coming and, to Anson's dismay, he found that his foremast was broken above the upper deck partners and held together by the fishes only.  In the process of clearing the ship below they were at last able to come at the leak which had given so much anxiety.  It was caused by a rotted bolt in a scarf of the stem below the 15-foot mark.

*At drinking they were expert*

On 22nd February they commenced heaving down and, after some trouble with the stretching of the tackle, the job of paying and sheathing the bottom was finished on 3rd March. They were delighted to find that underwater the ship was in very good condition. During the time of careening, a ship was of course easy prey for an enemy should he discover it. Anson learnt later that the Spanish Governor of Manilla, hearing that *Centurion* was at Typa, approved a scheme to burn her whilst careening, but his perfidy over the payment to the captain who was to do the deed resulted in the whole idea being dropped.

As soon as *Centurion* was upright once more her guns and their stores were got back on board in quick time and the foremast was repaired as fast as the work could be carried out. Even so it was the beginning of April before *Centurion* was completely renovated and ready to resume her voyage. The Chinese had shown extreme anxiety to hasten her departure, not knowing that Anson was just as keen to go as they were to see him gone. When two mandarins came aboard to urge his speedy departure he promptly told them to save their breath at which the Chinese, taking umbrage, cut off all supplies of food.

On 6th April, 1743, they left Typa and by the 18th were in Macao roads topping up their water casks as they went along. On the 19th *Centurion* at last got away to sea.

*Centurion surrounded by fishing boats*

# 18

# The Galleon Captured

ANSON HAD enrolled twenty-three Lascars and Dutch sailors to reinforce his complement. He let it be known on leaving Macao that he was bound for Batavia and on to England, although the westerly monsoon had set in. At this time such a passage was reckoned impracticable: yet he had persuaded both his own men and the people of Macao that his ship and his crew were equal to such an experiment. Many letters were put aboard at Macao for friends in Batavia.

In fact, ever since leaving Mexico Anson had been turning over in his mind a project which, now that he was well clear of the coast, he put to the ship's company. It was the first intimation of his intentions that any of them had. He called the entire crew to the quarter-deck and informed them that, instead of sailing for England, he intended to cruise for two Manilla galleons. The Squadron had prevented one from sailing in the previous year, from which it was reasonable to suppose that two galleons would sail from Acapulco in 1743. He planned to intercept them before they reached Manilla. He knew that they would carry about 500 hands and forty-four guns each, while his own numbers amounted to a mere 227 of whom thirty were boys. However, if his men fought with their usual spirit he was sure that at least one galleon could be taken. The response to this speech was immediate. The whole crew went wild with excitement and answered Anson with three good cheers. Once more the opportunity of capturing one of the great treasure vessels was being presented to them and their spirits soared with their impatience to get to grips with the Spaniards. The merry jingle of Spanish dollars in their pockets was the finest music they could think of—a fitting finale to the tattoo that they should play on the galleon's fat ribs.

*Centurion* stood to the eastward. On 1st May they saw Formosa and on the 20th were about 30 miles from Cape Esperitu Santo on Samar in the Philippines. Anson kept the ship well out of sight of land as this was the area in which he proposed to wait for the galleons and he knew that watchers kept a look-out from the Cape. All hands were in a fever of excitement for it was about this time that the galleons could be expected. The hardships they had suffered could with any luck at all be richly compensated by a glorious capture. The whole company was regularly exercised at the guns and small arms. In musketry some men were expert in marksmanship and rapid loading, for throughout the long voyage, whenever the opportunity occurred, Anson had consistently practised his men at their weapons, using only the cartridge method and aiming at a mark hanging from the yard arm. The ship was made ready for action and to avoid hampering the gunners the long-boat was hoisted out and lashed alongside.

Although Anson took every precaution to avoid being seen from the land, he later learned that they had been observed more than once. The news that the *Centurion* was in the area was sent to Manilla where it was at first disbelieved, but on further reports coming in the merchants of that city took fright and applied to the Governor for help. His Excellency agreed to fit out a force of two thirty-two-gun ships, one twenty-gun ship and two ten-gun sloops provided that the merchants footed the bill. But the principal ship was not ready for such an operation, the monsoon was against them, and Governor and merchants disagreed. The project was dropped.

A month after Anson's arrival on the station the look-out saw at sunrise a sail far off in the south-east. There was no sign of a second ship, but the crew assumed that one must still be below the horizon: they had no doubt that the ship in sight was their quarry. With his men tense and excited at their action stations Anson headed straight towards her and half an hour later the galleon fired a gun and took in her topgallant sails, which was presumed to be a signal to the consort. *Centurion* fired a gun to leeward, as Walter puts it, 'to amuse her'. Anson was surprised to find that the galleon made no attempt to alter her course but came steadily on towards the English ship. He did not at this time believe that *Centurion* had been recognised, but, in fact, the Spaniards realised that this was an English ship and were resolved to fight.

By noon the two vessels were some 3 miles apart and *Centurion* was well able to close with her opponent. There was still no sign of the second ship. The galleon in front of them was the *Nuestra Señora Cabadonga*, commanded by Don Jeronimo de Montero. Very shortly she hauled up her foresail and brought-to under topsails, with her bows to the north. The English were able to estimate the strength of their antagonist which from a distance appeared to be a much larger ship than *Centurion*, although it was not until the fight was over that they discovered what the differences were. The galleon hoisted Spanish colours and the Royal Standard of Spain flew from the main topgallant mast-head.

During the weeks of waiting Anson had rehearsed the crew of the *Centurion* in the tactics he intended to employ, a plan of action designed to make the most effective use of his armament with his limited numbers. About thirty men, picked for their reliability and marksmanship, were sent into the tops with muskets. As there were insufficient hands to man each gun completely, Anson allowed two men to each weapon for loading while he divided the rest into parties of ten or twelve men each whose job was to move along the decks and to run out and fire the guns as they became ready. Loaded muskets were laid on the gratings for those of the guns' crews to use when the time served because when the great guns were being loaded only the two men were employed at the business. By this method, although broadsides were not possible, every gun would be kept in action. It had a further advantage. Anson knew that the Spaniards were trained to lie flat on the deck when they saw a broadside being prepared and once it had been delivered they would get up and carry on with their own guns until they saw the next lot coming. His system of intermittent firing would effectively counter these safety measures.

Occasional squalls of rain hid the two ships from each other, but whenever the weather cleared the galleon was to be seen still lying-to and waiting. About one o'clock *Centurion* hoisted her broad pennant and colours. Being now within gun-shot of the enemy, it was possible to see that the Spaniards were belatedly throwing overboard cattle and lumber and clearing for the fight. Anson ordered his chase guns to fire a few rounds to annoy the enemy in his preparations. The galleon replied with her stern chase guns at which *Centurion* laid her splitsail yard fore and aft to facilitate possible boarding and the Spaniard immediately copied her. Soon after, *Centurion* came abreast of the enemy, a pistol-shot to leeward to prevent her opponent from running off before the wind.

The fight now began in earnest and for half an hour Anson lay ahead of the galleon where by the greater width of his ports he was

able to traverse all his guns whereas the Spaniard could bring only a
few of his weapons to bear.   Very early in the engagement the mats
which the galleon's crew had stuffed in the hammock nettings for
protection against musket balls caught fire and burnt violently,
blazing as high as the mizen top.   Whatever the fears of the Spaniards, Anson must have been equally anxious in case his prize should
go up in flames or—nearly as unwelcome—that the blazing ship
might easily drift against his own with disastrous results.   Luckily,
the Spaniards managed to tip the burning mass overboard, for which
no doubt thanks were offered up by both sides.

   *Centurion* stayed in the position which gave her such an advantage
and continued to sweep the galleon's decks with her guns and with
small arms fire from the tops.   The first volley from the English
muskets cleared all the enemy from the *Cabadonga*'s tops and the
marines then proceeded to pick off every officer who showed himself
on the quarter-deck of the Spanish ship including their General.
The training which Anson had given to his men in musketry proved
its worth.   Only one of the officers who appeared on the galleon's
quarter-deck escaped from their fire.

   The *Centurion* now drifted alongside the galleon.   Her gunners
fired steadily for another hour until grape-shot sweeping the decks
broke the Spanish discipline and will to resist, and their General lost
direction of the fight.   In the final stage of the battle the two vessels
drifted so close together that the Spanish officers could be seen endeavouring to prevent their men from deserting their posts.   Their
efforts were in vain.   After firing five or six guns aimed with some
care they at last surrendered and struck the standard at the main.
The ensign at the stern had already been burned from its staff.

   So *Centurion* at last accomplished the mission which she had
begun some eighteen months before.   In the action she lost only two
men killed, and a lieutenant and sixteen men wounded, one of whom
died later.   The Spaniards lost sixty dead and some seventy
wounded.

   The two ships were not in fact equally matched.   The *Cabadonga*
was the smaller, with a gun-deck 20 feet shorter than that of *Centurion*: her 700 tons was about 300 less than her opponent's.   The
Spanish ship was pierced for sixty-four guns, but she only carried
forty-four at the time, twelve of which were in the hold or lying un-
mounted on deck.   Her basic design was that of a trading ship,
lacking the high bulwarks of a warship to protect the men on deck,
and her small gunports limited the traverse of her guns of which
Anson took such full advantage.   The Spaniards had, however,
great superiority in numbers—530 persons in all or more than double
the *Centurion*'s complement, but a large part of these must be

reckoned as non-combatant. She was carrying a crew of 266 and also forty soldiers, the remainder being passengers, servants or convicts and of these not many can have been of any use in a naval action.

The *Nuestra Señora de Cabadonga* was a rich prize worth near a million and a half dollars. After eighteen months of disappointment the crew of the *Centurion* were jubilant at their capture, an immense treasure that promised wealth for all, but even at this last minute they came perilously close to losing everything. A lieutenant, under cover of congratulating Anson on his victory, informed him that the *Centurion* was on fire dangerously near the powder magazine. Anson gave no indication to the bystanders that anything was amiss. Quietly and efficiently a fire party brought the flames under control.

Saumarez was made captain of the prize. All the Spaniards were sent aboard *Centurion* except for those needed to help the prize crew. Anson asked for news of the second galleon and was told that she had left Acapulco much earlier than the *Cabadonga* and had probably arrived at Manilla long before he had reached Esperitu Santo. The long delays at Macao had robbed the English of half their expectations. Nevertheless, their capture was rich enough to satisfy even the most covetous.

No time was lost in transferring the treasure from the prize to *Centurion*, which Anson considered the safer ship. He decided to return to Canton. The prisoners presented a serious problem as they outnumbered his own men by two to one. When they came aboard and saw the large proportion of boys amongst the victors, they were shocked and the commander of the *Cabadonga*, according to John Philips, actually broke down and wept at the disgrace. To safeguard his ship against a rising Anson confined all his captives in the hold, except for the officers and the wounded, leaving the hatches open for air. Wooden funnels were erected between the hatches of the upper and lower decks to provide forced ventilation for the unfortunate men in the hold. Although the Spaniards could not have climbed the smooth interior of these funnels, four swivel guns loaded with musket shot were placed at the mouth of each as a precaution against a rising.

Thomas was one of the prize crew on the *Cabadonga* and tells an unpleasant story of the Spanish General who was now set at liberty. '. . . He was not only allowed the use of his own cabin till he should be recovered of his wound, but obtained the services of an English surgeon; Anson, at the same time, sending an officer to demand his commission. The General made the officer look in the locker of his private cabin, where he said the commission would be found, along with a sword-belt studded with diamonds of great value; and when the box was found empty, the Spaniard averred that some of the English, rummaging in his cabin, must have stolen and secreted the contents.  Despite the non-production of his commission, the General received the most humane and liberal treatment, being allowed at his departure to carry off several chests and trunks unsearched which he claimed as his private property, though he had many valuable ventures concealed which should have been given up as fair and lawful prize.'

Persisting to the last in the assertion of the theft of his commission and sword-belt, he brought down on the prize crew a heavy and undeserved punishment; for Anson, on their arrival in the Canton river, absolutely prohibited their intercourse with the natives, that the thief might have no chance of parting with his booty undiscovered.  Thomas, however, was afterwards told at Macao by an Irish priest that the General retained both his commission and his swordbelt; that he had made no secret of his fraud; and that he had offered the diamonds—which were made up in the belt by way of a blind—among the merchants at Macao for sale.

Among the prisoners also, so Thomas records, was an old gentleman, the Governor of Guam who was going to Manilla to renew his commission and who had scarce mounted the *Centurion*'s side before he was received with open arms by Mr. Crooden, captain of marines, who thirty-six years before, at the battle of Almanza, had been his prisoner and honourably used by him.  These two renewed their old acquaintance and Crooden had a long-wished-for opportunity of returning the favours he had formerly received and which he gratefully remembered.

The seventeen officers were put in a cabin under a constant guard of six men.  It was understood that any violence or disturbance would be punished by death and all the *Centurion*'s crew were armed; the officers never took their clothes off and slept with their weapons at hand.  But the plight of the prisoners was ghastly, as very little could be done for them.  The weather was terribly hot, the stink from the hold 'loathsome beyond all conception' and their allowance of water just sufficient to keep them alive.  *Centurion*'s crew had a pint and a half a day per man—the prisoners had a pint.  In spite of these shocking conditions only three of the wounded men died, but the rest were reduced to living skeletons.

Twenty days after the fight they anchored once more off Macao.  The galleon had yielded 1,313,843 pieces of eight, 35,682 oz. of pure silver, and some other valuables of less consequence.  The *Cabadonga* was Anson's last prize.  The total value of the coin, plate, precious metal and other forms of treasure taken during the voyage came to nearly £400,000—a gigantic sum in those days.  In addition the

ships and merchandise burnt or destroyed by Anson's Squadron
were conservatively reckoned at another £600,000.  A total loss to
the Spanish nation of over a million sterling; and this calculation
takes no account of the formidable cost to the Spanish Government
of Pizarro's ill-fated expedition.  There was no possible doubt of
the success of the expedition, which had triumphantly accomplished
the objectives assigned to it in spite of the terrible loss of life and
ships.  Anson's own leadership was beyond praise.

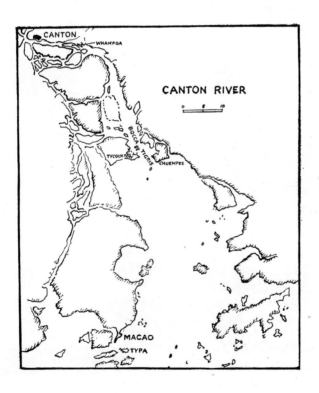

*Cabadonga's* mats
*catch fire*

# 19

# A Safe Return

CENTURION CAME finally to anchor below the Bocca Tigris and very shortly an officer of the Mandarin came off in a boat to examine the two ships. Anson gave him the information that he required, explaining that he would shelter in the Canton river until the hurricane season was over.

The officer then wanted an account of the men, guns and ammunition on board, for the information of the Government at Canton. But when he learnt that there were in *Centurion* 400 muskets and between 300 and 400 barrels of powder he was scared stiff and cried out that no ship ever came into Canton river armed like that. He said he dared not write all this down lest it should frighten the Regency! However, he intended to leave two custom house officers behind him to ensure that *Centurion* did not leave without paying dues. Anson replied that, as he commanded a man-o'-war, he was not allowed to meddle in trading or concern himself with customs or duties, but out of deference to the Chinese authorities he would allow the two men aboard. The officer, recovering himself, told the Commodore that duty must be paid by all ships coming into the Emperor's ports, and at the same time gave secret instructions to the Chinese pilot not to take the English ship through the Bocca Tigris.

The Bocca Tigris is a narrow passage formed by two points of land each of which was fortified. On one side there was a battery at the waterside, in which twelve iron cannon, 4- or 6-pounders, were mounted although there were embrasures for eighteen. A rocky spur on the other side of the strait was topped by a castle with about ten 6-pounders. These two defences were all that the Chinese thought necessary to secure the passage, but, of course, they formed no deterrent whatever. Anson ordered the pilot to take the ship through immediately—the bad weather acting as a spur—and to stimulate his zeal threatened him with instant death if the ship ran aground. The pilot did his job safely, the forts offering no resistance. But when the poor fellow returned on shore the Chinese authorities had him soundly thrashed and put in prison. Later he found a way to meet Anson and asked compensation for the punishment he had suffered in the Commodore's business and Anson gave him such a sum of money as would at any time have enticed a Chinese to undergo a dozen bastinadoings. Indeed, he was not the only official in trouble. The mandarin who had issued instructions barring the British ship from the channel was to be severely punished for allowing the ships to pass. Anson intervened, pointing out that neither the forts nor anything else could have stopped him, with which opinion the Chinese agreed, but said that the mandarin must nevertheless be dealt with for not having done the impossible.

On 16th July Anson sent his Second Lieutenant to the Viceroy at Canton explaining why it was necessary to bring *Centurion* into port, and informing His Excellency of the Commodore's intention to pay him a visit in the immediate future. Meantime Anson allowed several Spanish officers of the *Cabadonga* two days' leave on parole. On their arrival at Canton they were sent for and examined especially on the matter of the capture of the galleon. They told an honest story, that as the two countries were at war they had decided to capture the British ship and had borne down on her with that intention, but were defeated. They told of their treatment as prisoners by Anson and how much better it was by comparison with what they should have dealt him had the position been reversed. At this the Chinese were obviously agreeably surprised for they had up to this point thought of the Commodore more as a freebooter than a King's officer on his lawful business. But now of course he was an important person: and had he not got a vast treasure in his hands of which, by diplomatic and Oriental persuasion, a few taels might be jiggled their way?

*The Bocca Tigris*

The authorities were clearly not absolutely satisfied over two things which the Spaniards had told them and on these points they asked for further explanation.   The one was the vast disparity of numbers between the *Cabadonga* and the *Centurion,* and secondly the humane treatment meted to them by a conqueror.   How came the Spanish to be beaten by such an inferior force, and why were they not put to death when captured ?   The reply to the first question was that *Centurion* was a ship of war with greater guns and superior in many ways to the galleon.   As to the killing of prisoners, this was not done to those who submitted, but they said, the Commodore from his nature had treated them and their countrymen who had formerly been in his power, with a humanity not required from a victor and rarely practised by nations at war.   These remarks turned the Chinese opinion greatly in favour of Anson.

On 20th July in the small hours, three mandarins with a great number of boats and people came to the *Centurion* and Anson received from them the Viceroy's order for a daily supply of pro- visons and for pilots to conduct the ships up river as far as the second bar.   The Viceroy also sent his reply to Anson's letter excusing himself from receiving the Commodore owing to the heat of the weather and the inconvenience it would cause to assemble the mandarins and soldiers for the ceremony.   He would be pleased to see him in September when the weather would be cooler.   Anson was well aware that this delay was only to gain time for the Viceroy who wished to have the Emperor's instructions in the matter.

When these messages had been read, the mandarins began to talk of the duties to be paid by the ships, but the Commodore cut them short with a prompt but decided refusal to pay any duties whatever. The Chinese then mentioned another matter—and that concerned the Spanish prisoners.   The Viceroy felt that the Emperor might be displeased by the idea of friendly nationals being confined as pri- soners in his dominions.   Would Anson therefore release them ? Only too delighted to have them off his hands the Commodore at first raised some difficulties, but let himself be persuaded.   To please the Viceroy he would release the prisoners just as soon as boats were sent to collect them.   Two junks were sent and the Purser was ordered to supply them with eight days' provisions for the journey down river to Macao.   This delicate matter being satis- factorily settled, *Centurion* was at last permitted to come to moorings above the second bar, to stay there until the monsoon was past.

From now on Anson was to suffer continual annoyance from the fraudulent tricks of which the Orientals are masters.   Although the daily supplies of food were always brought aboard, the sea stores for the journey home did not materialise.   From the Viceroy downwards every man with whom they had to deal lied to them consistently. Promises of delivery were never kept, and no one stuck to his contracts. One of *Centurion*'s officers taking a convalescent walk on shore was robbed and beaten up. Mandarins (they seem to sprout up from every sentence in Walter's book) came with protestations at the affair and promises to bring the culprit to justice; but of course they were all in league and, in fact, one of them had instigated the theft.

A topmast, which Anson had borrowed at Macao, was stolen and a reward paid for its recovery. The Chinese interpreter was to pay it to the Mandarin who had found the spar. Naturally he put the money in his own pocket, but was caught later and dismissed. He came whining to Anson for reinstatement saying: 'Chinese man very great rogue truly, but have fashion no can help.'

The list of tricks and frauds is endless. To the Chinese the English must have appeared as a gift from Heaven sent for their especial benefit: and it is impossible not to be amused when reading the stories of their practices. The established Chinese method of buying and selling all things by weight naturally meant that where the weight could be supplemented at no cost to the seller then the profit to him would increase. A large quantity of fowls and ducks were sold to *Centurion* of which the majority promptly died. The crew naturally thought the birds had been killed by poison, but when they were examined it was found that they were filled with stones and gravel—about ten ounces in each bird! In the same fashion, hogs which had been bought ready killed had been injected full of water so that when hung up to drain overnight a carcass lost about a stone in weight. To stop this particular cheating orders were given for the hogs to be bought alive—but the Chinese were quite equal to the situation. They fed the hogs a quantity of water. By simple but cruel means the poor animals were prevented from urinating and were sold in a bloated and tortured condition. As these same fellows had no objection to eating anything that had died, they made certain that some of the livestock should die soon after delivery and then be thrown overboard. And two-thirds of the hogs did die before *Centurion* was out of sight of land and many Chinese boats were following just to pick up the carcasses.

By the end of September the Commodore was tired of being continually fobbed off with lies and false promises whenever he mentioned provisions. On 27th September he sent a message to the Mandarin to say that he wished to see the Viceroy. He would go to Canton on 1st October and the day after he arrived he wished the Viceroy to fix a time for audience. Anson intended to pay his call in style. The boat's crew were dressed in excellent uniforms very like that of the Thames Watermen. There were eighteen of them and a coxswain; they had scarlet jackets and blue silk waistcoats, the whole trimmed with silver buttons and with silver badges on their jackets and caps.

It was a fair guess that the dues would be demanded before any permit for victualling the ship would be issued.

The Chinese merchants of course were in a dilemma. They were responsible for the behaviour, and prompt payment of customs dues, of any foreign devil with whom they traded and Anson's refusal to pay any duties whatever was to them a serious breach of trading arrangements. One can sympathise with the Hong merchants who were torn between their desire to do business with the English and the certain punishment by the Viceroy if the dues were not paid.

But perhaps more serious was the loss of face which the Emperor would suffer if Anson got away with it. Unfortunately for His Celestial Majesty's representative *Centurion* presented a sixty-gun argument that was very difficult to oppose.

The Commodore was never going to dishonour his flag by paying taxes for the King's ship, but he realised that the Chinese might attempt to trap him. Accordingly, he appointed Mr. Brett to be Captain of the *Centurion* while he was away and gave instructions that, if the Commodore was detained in consequence of the dispute over the dues, he was to take the men out of the *Cabadonga*, destroy the ship, and then to go down river through the Bocca Tigris with *Centurion*. Once outside the strait Brett was to wait until he received further orders.

The Chinese quickly recognised Anson's determination and also that even if they used violence they would get nothing from him. The loss of face was hard to bear, more so perhaps than the loss of dues, but there was nothing they could do about it. But neither were they able to play straight with Anson. A letter was received saying that the Viceroy desired Anson to delay his visit for two or three days. This was followed in the afternoon by a message that the Viceroy had expected him that same day. The troops had been assembled, the reception committee was waiting and the disappointment was general. The Viceroy, it was said, had imprisoned Anson's interpreter, and the whole affair was adroitly worked up

*The Barge Crew*

into pressure on Anson's nerves and patience, a subtle game in which even foreign influence was brought into play. The super-cargoes of all the English ships lying at Canton sent him a letter expressing their fear that some insult would be offered him should he come to Canton before the Viceroy had satisfied himself about the whole business. To this Anson replied that he believed the entire affair to be bluff intended to frighten him into acquiescence. So— he would go to Canton on 13th October confident that there would be no nonsense from the Chinese who now knew what they could expect. On 13th October, therefore, his barge with the super-cargoes of all the English, Danish and Swedish ships on board left for Canton accompanied by his own and the boats from the trading ships. As they passed by Whampo where the European ships lay they were saluted by all except the French vessels.

On his arrival the Commodore was greeted by the principal merchants who assured him that as soon as the Viceroy knew he was in Canton—and they would inform him the next morning—a meeting would immediately be arranged. As usual, on the next day there were excuses and stories of it being impossible for them to gain any admittance to the Viceroy and the visit must wait, all of which Anson knew to be lies. But he was in no hurry and agreed to wait—with one proviso. If, when his sea stores were ready to be shipped in forty days' time, the merchants had not arranged an interview, Anson would conduct his own business without them. The Chinese raised objections and swore they would do nothing until Anson paid in advance for everything he had ordered. He calmly ignored this threat and settled down to wait.

On 24th November his stores were ready to be shipped but still no meeting had been arranged. He was at last free to act without relying on intermediaries and so sent an officer to the Mandarin in charge of the guard at the chief gate of the city, with a letter to the Viceroy. In preparing this letter Anson employed a Mr. Flint, who was in the service of the East India Company, a man who had been in China for many years and spoke Chinese perfectly. This done, he resumed his vigil.

Two days after the dispatch of the letter a fire broke out in the suburbs of the city. Anson immediately went with his officers and

*Canton*

boat's crew to do what he could to help. By pulling down buildings to isolate the outbreak the English were slowly getting the flames under control when they were informed that, as no Mandarin was directing operations, Anson would be responsible for the cost of any destruction his men might do. At this they stopped and transferred their services as fire-fighters to the East India Company's factory. The Chinese could only stand and look on, occasionally holding an idol up to the flames, until at last a Mandarin and some four or five hundred fireman arrived, but achieved nothing. As the fire began to take a real hold, threatening to engulf the whole city, the Viceroy himself, realising that he would soon be master of an ash heap, sent a formal request to Anson for help and authorised him to take any action he thought fit.

So once again English tars started to tear down houses and buildings, going at it like children, falling off roofs and collapsing in the middle of ruins and thoroughly enjoying themselves at the trivial cost of some bruises. But they put the fire out! The Chinese could only look on in amazement at such vigour.

The conflagration while it lasted did enormous damage. One merchant was said to have lost 200,000 sterling. Other merchants came to the Commodore and asked for men to guard their warehouses and dwellings, because they were likely to lose as much by robbery as fire. In the morning many of the principal officers came to thank Anson for what he had done and for saving their city. The Viceroy too at last sent a message fixing the date of meeting as 30th November which in gratitude was the least he could do under the circumstances. It was going to be easy to get the licence now, whereas but for his services in the fire Anson would have been opposed at every turn.

At ten on the morning of the appointed day, being informed of the Viceroy's pleasure, Anson and his people set off for the city. At the outer gate was a guard of 200 soldiers drawn up to attend him and they conducted him to the Emperor's Palace. In front of it were paraded 10,000 troops under arms, who presented a splendid sight, dressed in new uniforms. Anson and his party passed through them to where the Viceroy was seated under a rich canopy in the Emperor's chair of state with the whole Council of Mandarins attendant. A seat was provided for Anson. He was ranked third in order from the Viceroy. Only the Head of the Law and the Treasurer—who in China at that time took precedence over all military personnel—were ranked above him.

The preliminaries being over, Anson gave an account of the attempts to get an audience of the Viceroy, the continual frustrations and his final personal letter to the Viceroy delivered at the gate of the

12

palace. Here the Viceroy stopped the interpreter—Mr. Flint before mentioned—and asked that Mr. Anson be informed that his letter was the first intimation he had had that the Commodore was at Canton. Anson then proceeded to report that British subjects trading to China had complained to him of the vexatious impositions by the Chinese merchants and by inferior Custom House officers, to which they were compelled to submit because they were never able to gain access to the mandarins who could grant them redress. As an officer of His Majesty King George the Second it was his duty to put these grievances before the Viceroy, that orders should be given to prevent any further reasons for complaint. Here Anson paused, waiting for an answer from the Viceroy. Nothing being said, the Commodore inquired from the interpreter if the Viceroy had fully heard and understood what he had asked. Mr. Flint assured him that he had been understood all right but that there was unlikely to be any reply.

Anson then put the case of the ship *Haslingfield* which having been dismasted on the coast had arrived at Canton a few days before. The fire had done great damage to her and her people; her Captain in particular having lost all his goods in the flames and in the tumult had a chest of cash to the tune of 4,500 taels stolen by Chinese boat-

*Anson received by the Viceroy*

men.   He asked for the Government's help as it was obvious that the money would never be recovered without the orders from the mandarins.   The Viceroy said that in settling the Emperor's customs for that ship, some rebate should be made for her losses.

Anson had dealt with the business which the officers of the East India Company had entrusted to him and now entered on his own affairs.   The time and weather, he said, had now come for him to return to Europe, for which he only required the licence to embark his provisions and stores.   As soon as it should be granted and the goods shipped on board, he would leave the river at once.   The Viceroy answered that the licence should be immediately issued and everything ordered on board the following day.   He thanked the Commodore for his great services at the fire and the saving of the city, and then noted that the *Centurion* had been in Chinese waters a good while.   (Was he still hankering for dues?)   Nevertheless he wished Anson a good voyage.   The Commodore thanked him and took his leave.   This ended a four-month battle against chicanery and deception which, but for his actions in the fire, might conceivably have had a different conclusion.   What pleased him most, however, was the precedent he had created by which H.M. ships were exempted from all demands of duty in any Chinese port.   As he left the city he was saluted with three guns which were the most ever fired for such an occasion.

*The Home-coming*

On 1st December the provisions began to arrive on board and four days later Anson embarked at Canton for the *Centurion*. On the 7th the two ships unmoored and sailed down river. They passed through the Bocca Tigris and noted that the two forts were now crammed full with men, most of whom were armed with pikes and match-lock muskets. The men marched about with much pomp, to impress Anson no doubt, and there were lots of flags and heaps of gun stones. A very large soldier stalked about on the parapet with a battleaxe in his hand dressed in splendid armour—made of silver paper!

On 12th December the ships once more anchored off Macao and, whilst there, merchants offered Anson 6,000 dollars for the *Nuestra Señora de Cabadonga*, a price which was far below her value. The Chinese knew of the Commodore's anxiety to get to sea and no doubt were certain of a bargain. The war with Spain was still continuing and Anson had learnt from the East Indiamen that France might enter against Britain before he could arrive home. Obviously no knowledge of his capture of the galleon could possibly get to Europe until the Indiamen returned and so he determined to be the messenger of his own good fortune. So he accepted the merchants' offer. On 15th December, 1742, *Centurion* set sail for England.

On 3rd January, 1743, *Centurion* anchored in the straits of Sunda, wooding and watering until the 8th when she set a course for the Cape of Good Hope and anchored in Table Bay on 11th March. Here they stayed until the beginning of April refreshing men and replenishing stores. Anson enlisted some forty new men before sailing on 3rd April. The 19th saw them passing St. Helena and on 10th June they spoke with an English ship from Amsterdam which gave them the first news that France had entered the war. On the 12th they saw the Lizard and three days later came to anchor in Spithead. On their arrival they heard that they had narrowly

missed, thanks to dense fog, a French fleet cruising in the chops of the channel: a most fortunate fog if ever there was one.

The epic voyage ended after three years and nine months. On her return to England *Centurion* had on board 145 of the original company which had manned the expedition's five ships in 1741. Only four men had died by enemy action; more than 1,300 from disease and the hazards of the sea.

The Government, indeed the whole country, were jubilant at Anson's triumph and in London the *Centurion*'s crew were given a tumultuous reception. On 5th July, the *General Advertiser* reported:

> Yesterday the money taken by Admiral Anson was carried through the City in thirty-two wagons, preceded by a kettle-drum, trumpets, and French horns guarded by the seamen, commanded by the Officers richly dressed, and was lodged in the Tower. On the first wagon was the English colours, with the Spanish ensign under it, and every third or fourth wagon carried some trophy of honour, which had been taken from the Spaniards in the South Sea, as well as from the Acapulco ship. Their Royal Highnesses the Prince and Princess of Wales, and Admiral Anson, were at a house in Pall Mall to see the procession.

In a sense this procession marked the end of Anson's expedition. He and his men had triumphed over great hardships and won public acclaim that was well deserved. For the crew their achievements brought temporary affluence which some of them celebrated not wisely but too well (Appendix VII).

The voyage established Anson's reputation for all time. He received immediate promotion to rear-admiral—the first step in a long and distinguished career as a commander and at the Admiralty. No fewer than eight of his young officers were destined to win flag rank in later years (Appendix IV) and this success was in large measure due to the schooling they received from one of the finest seamen that England has produced.

*Appendices*

# Appendix I

## H.M. INSTRUCTIONS FOR MR. ANSON

Instructions for our trusty and well-beloved George Anson, Esq., Commander-in-Chief of our ships designed to be sent into the South Seas in America. Given at our Court at St. James's the 31st day of January, 1739–40, in the thirteenth year of our reign.

Whereas we have thought proper to declare war against The King of Spain, for the several injuries and indignities offered to our Crown and people, which are more particularly set forth in our declaration of war, we have thought fit to direct that you, taking under your command our ships, should proceed with them according to the following instructions.

You are to receive on board our said ships five hundred of our land forces, and to proceed forthwith to the Cape de Verde Islands, and to supply your ships with water and such refreshments as are to be procured there; and you are from thence to make the best of your way to the Island of St. Catherine, on the coast of Brazil, or such other place on that coast as you may be advised is more proper, where you are again to supply your ships with water and any other necessaries you may want that can be had there. And when you have done so, you are to proceed with our ships under your command into the South Sea, either round Cape Horn or through the Streights of Magellan, as you shall judge most proper, and according as the season of the year and winds and weather shall best permit.

When you shall arrive on the Spanish coast of the South Sea, you are to use your best endeavours to annoy and distress the Spaniards, either at sea or land, to the utmost of your power, by taking, sinking, burning, or otherwise destroying all their ships and vessels that you shall meet with, and particularly their boats, and all embarkations whatsoever, that they may not be able to send any intelligence by sea along the coast of your being in those parts.

In case you shall find it practical to seize, surprise or take any of the towns or places belonging to the Spaniards on the coast, that you may judge worthy of making such an enterprize upon, you are to attempt it: for which purpose we have not only ordered the land forces above mentioned, but have also thought proper to direct that an additional number of small arms be put on board the ships under your command to be used, as occasion may require, by the crews of the said ships, or otherwise, as you shall find best for our service. And you are, on such occasions, to take the opinion of the Captains of our ships under your command at a Council of War: of which Council of War, in case of any attack or enterprise by land, the commander of our land forces shall also be one; which said land forces shall, upon such occasions, be landed according to the determination of the said Council of War. And as it will be absolutely necessary for you to be supplied with provisions and water, when and where they can be had, you will inform yourself of the places where that can most conveniently be done; and as we have been informed that the coasts of Chile, and particularly the island of Chilloe, do abound with provisions and necessaries of all sorts, you are to call there for that purpose.

As it has been represented unto us that the number of native Indians on the coast of Chile greatly exceeds that of the Spaniards, and that there is reason to believe that the said Indians may not be averse to join with you against the Spaniards in order to recover their freedom, you are to endeavour to cultivate a good understanding with such Indians as shall be willing to join and assist you in any attempt that you may think proper to make against the Spaniards that are established there.

You are to continue your voyage along the coast of Peru, and to get the best information you can whether there be any place before you come to Lima that may be worthy your attention, so as to make it advisable to stop at it. But if there be no place where any considerable advantage can be expected, you are then to go along the coast till you come to Callao, which is the port of Lima, taking or destroying all embarkations whatsoever that you shall meet with.

As soon as you shall arrive at Callao you shall consider whether it may be practicable to make an attempt upon that place or not; and if it shall be judged practicable by a Council of War, to be held for that purpose, with the strength you have with you to make an attempt upon that port, you are accordingly to do it. And if it shall please God to bless our arms with success you are then to endeavour to turn it to the best advantage possible for our service.

And whereas there is some reason to believe from private intelligence that the Spaniards in the kingdom of Peru, and especially in that part of it which is near Lima, have long had an inclination to revolt from their obedience to the King of Spain (on account of the great oppressions and tyrannies exercised by the Spanish Vice-Roys and Governors) in favour of some considerable person among themselves, you are, if you find that there is any foundation for these reports, by all possible means to encourage and assist such a design in the best manner you shall be able. And in case of any revolution or revolt from the obedience of the King of Spain, either among the Spaniards or the Indians in those parts, and of any new government being erected by them, you are to insist upon the most advantageous conditions for the commerce of our subjects, to be carried on with such government so to be erected; for which purpose you shall make provisional agreements, subject to our future approbation and confirmation.

But, in case you should not think proper to attack Callao, or should miscarry in any attempt you may make against that place, you are then to proceed to the northward, as far as Panama.

But as there are many places along the coast which are considerable, and where the Spanish ships in their passage between Panama and Lima do usually stop, it will be proper for you to look into those places, and to annoy Spaniards there, as much as it shall be in your power. And if you

13

shall meet with the Spanish men-o'-war that carry the treasure from Lima to Panama, you are to endeavour to make yourself master of them.

When you are arrived at Panama you will probably have an opportunity to take or destroy such embarkations as you shall find there. And as the town itself is represented to be not very strong, especially as it has been lately burnt down, you are, if you shall think you have sufficient force for that purpose, to make an attempt upon that town and endeavour to take it, or burn and destroy it, as you think most for our service.

And as you may possibly find an opportunity to send privately overland to Portobello or Darien, you are by that means to endeavour to transmit to any of our ships or forces that shall be on that coast an account of what you have done, or intend to do. And lest any such intelligence should fall into the hands of the Spaniards we have ordered you to be furnished with a cipher in which manner only you are to correspond with our Admiral, or the Commander-in-Chief of any of our ships, that may be in the northern seas of America, or the Commander-in-Chief of our land forces.

As we have determined to send a large body of troops from hence as early as possible in the spring to make a descent on some part of the Spanish West Indies, and as we shall have a very considerable fleet in those seas, in case it should be thought proper that any part of those ships or troops should go to Portobello or Darien with a design to send the said troops overland to Panama or Santa Maria, you are then to make the best disposition to assist them by all the means that you shall be able, in making a secure settlement either at Panama or any other place that shall be thought proper. And you are in such case to supply them with cannon from the ships under your command (if necessary), or with anything else that can be spared without much weakening the squadron. And if the land forces on board our said ships should be wanted to reinforce those that may come overland to the coast of the South Sea, you may cause them to go on shore for that purpose with the approbation of the proper officers.

When you shall have proceeded thus far it must in a great measure be left to your discretion, and that of a Council-of-War (when, upon any difficulty, you shall think fit to call them together) to consider whether you shall go further to the northward, or remain longer at Panama, in case the place should have been taken by our forces, or you can anyway hear that any of our forces may be expected on that side from the north side. But you will always take particular care to consider of a proper place for careening of the ships, and for supplying them with provisions, either for their voyage homeward, or for their continuing voyage abroad, for in case of your success more ships may be sent at a proper season of the year.

In case you shall be so happy as to meet with success you should take the first opportunity, by sending a ship on purpose, or otherwise, to acquaint us with it, and with every particular that may be necessary for us to be informed of, that we may take the proper measures thereupon.

If you shall find no occasion for your staying longer in those seas, and shall judge it best to go to the northward as far as Acapulco, or to look out for the Acapulco ship, which sails from that place for Manilla at a certain time of the year and generally returns at a certain time also, you may possibly in that case think it most advisable to return home by way of China, which you are hereby authorised to do, or as it is probable that it may be difficult to get a sufficient quantity of provision, and more probable to be supplied in Chile, to return home by Cape Horn, as you shall think best for our service, and for the preservation of the ships and the men on board them.

Whenever you shall judge it necessary for our service to return with our squadron to England you may, if you shall think it proper, leave one or two of our ships in the South Sea for the security of any of the acquisitions you may have been able to make for the protection of the trade which any of our subjects may be carrying on in those parts.

Whereas the season of the year is so far advanced that it may not be possible for you to arrive at Cape Horn, or to pass the Streights of Magellan before the navigation in those parts may be so dangerous that it cannot be attempted without risk to our squadron, you are in that case by no means to venture it, but to proceed directly to the River Plata, and there to remain till the season of the year shall permit you to go with safety to those seas.   And as there is no certain account that the rich ships that were to come from Buenos Aires are yet sailed from thence, it is possible that you may arrive time enough to intercept and take them, which in that case you will use your utmost endeavours to do.

During your stay in the River Plata you shall endeavour to annoy the Spaniards in the best manner you are able, as by taking, burning, sinking or otherwise destroying any ships or other embarkations that they may have there, as by taking or destroying any of the Spanish settlements and possessions which you may think practicable, to endeavour to take Montevideo, and demolish it, or put it into the possession of the Portuguese in case the Portuguese governor of Nova Colonia should by his behaviour encourage you to do so.   And whilst you are in the River Plata you will keep a good correspondence with the Portuguese Governor of Nova Colonia who, it is not doubted, will be willing to supply you with whatever provisions you may want for the service of our ships under your command.

When you shall have annoyed and destroyed the Spaniards as much as you shall be able in the River Plata you are then to proceed to the South Seas as soon as the season of the year will permit, either round Cape Horn or through the Streights of Magellan, and act according to the directions contained in the former part of these our instructions.

# Appendix II

# ADDITIONAL INSTRUCTIONS FOR
# MR. ANSON

By the Lords Justices additional instructions for George Anson Esq., Commander-in-Chief of His Majesty's ships to be sent into the South Seas in America. Given at Whitehall the 19th day of June 1740 in the fourteenth year of His Majesty's reign.

Whereas His Majesty was pleased to sign certain instructions, bearing date the 31st day of January 1739/40 directed to you, we have ordered the same to be herewith delivered to you, and have thought fit also to give you these additional instructions for your conduct.

His Majesty having been pleased to suspend your sailing from England till this time, when the season of the years will permit you to make your intended voyage directly to the South Seas in America (which at some particular seasons is extremely difficult, if not impracticable) you are now to proceed forthwith with His Majesty's ships under your command, directly to the South Seas, either by going round Cape Horn or through the Streights of Magellan, and to act according to the directions contained in His Majesty's instructions to you. But you are to regard that part of the said instructions where you was ordered (in case you should be too late for your passage to the South Seas) to proceed directly to the River Plata, and there remain till the season of the year should permit you to go with safety to the South Seas, to be at present out of the question, and of no force. And whereas you are directed by His Majesty's instructions to cause the land forces which are to go on board His Majesty's ships under your command to be put on shore, on one particular occasion, with the approbation of the proper officers, you are to understand it to be His Majesty's intention that the said land forces are in no case to be put on shore unless it shall be previously approved by a Council of War to be held for that purpose.

Whereas a letter wrote by the Governor of Panama to the King of Spain has fallen into the hands of some of His Majesty's officers, which letter contains very material advices relating to the situation of the Spaniards, and to the keeping of their treasure in those parts, a copy of the same will by our order be herewith put into your hands; and you are to have a regard to the intelligence therein contained in the execution of the orders given you in His Majesty's instructions.

In case of your inability by sickness or otherwise to execute His Majesty's orders, the officer next to you in rank is hereby authorised and directed to take upon him the command of His Majesty's ships that are to go with you, and to execute the orders contained in your instructions as if they were directed to himself.

# Appendix III

# *THE* SEVERN *AND THE* PEARL

The stories of the *Severn* and *Pearl* were not included in Walter's book. Little of their adventures had come to light beyond the fact that they had suffered even more than Anson, if that were possible. Captain Legge of the *Severn* in a letter to Josiah Burchett, Secretary of the Admiralty, described the trials of the *Severn* during the terribly stormy days of March and April when most of his men were sick and trying their hardest to repair their perished sails and rotten rigging. On 10th April, 1741, they lost sight of all the other ships except the *Pearl*. On 25th April the two ships lost sight of each other and contact was not regained until 21st May.

At a consultation on board the *Severn* between Legge and his officers it was decided to make an effort to return to some place where men and ships could be replenished and, after further severe weather, they turned back.

Legge says that he had endured almost continual storms for forty days with his sails and rigging in tatters. When he was at last able to speak with a Portuguese trading vessel he was horrified to discover that his estimated position was nearly 600 miles out. On 6th June he arrived with *Severn* at Rio de Janiero with hardly thirty men fit to work the ship, and these few barely able to walk the deck. Legge says that amongst other appointments he was compelled to make was that of William Bacon, boatswain's mate, to be cook. This man was seventy years old and had served in H.M. Ships as boatswain's mate for forty years.

At Rio they received kindly and humane treatment from the Portuguese authorities and from private people. As far as was possible every assistance and help towards putting his ship to rights was afforded him, but the prices of materials were too high to permit of refitting. It was hoped to get all necessary gear and men from England. *Severn* had only one maintopsail and one foresail fit to set: *Pearl* had no rigging or sails at all. In brief, the two ships were in no state to proceed and it was estimated that it would be two months before any man would be fit for duty.

The surgeon to the Portuguese army at Rio assured Legge that to put his men aboard ship on salt provisions before they were fully recovered would kill them.

On 2nd July Captain Murray complained to Legge at being held at Rio by that officer. Murray was of the opinion that he should endeavour to make his way round the Horn to try and reach Anson or else to take his ship to Barbados or some such place and perform useful service. Legge, as senior officer, was certain that the resources of the two ships together, reduced as they were by storm and disease, were insufficient to enable even one of them to undertake a voyage of any consequence. Eventually, however, on 5th February, 1742, the two ships arrived at Barbados.

## Appendix IV

# OFFICERS WITH ANSON WHO LATER ATTAINED FLAG RANK

PIERCY BRETT (1709–81), Admiral of the Blue, Lord Commissioner of the Admiralty. Knighted 1753.

The Hon. JOHN BYRON (1723–86), Vice-Admiral of the White, Governor of Newfoundland: grandfather of the poet.

JOHN CAMPBELL (1720–90), Vice-Admiral of the Red, Governor of the Newfoundland and Commander-in-Chief. Refused Knighthood 1759.

PETER DENIS (d. 1778), Admiral of the Red. Created Baronet 1767.

The Hon. AUGUSTUS KEPPEL (1725–86), Admiral of the White, First Lord of the Admiralty. Created Viscount Keppel 1782.

HYDE PARKER (1714–82), Vice-Admiral of the Red. Succeeded to Baronetcy 1782.

CHARLES SAUNDERS (1713–75), Admiral of the Blue, First Lord of the Admiralty. Knighted 1752. Victor with Wolfe at Quebec.

RICHARD HOWE (1726–99), Admiral of the Fleet and one of the great figures in the history of the Royal Navy, served in the *Severn* as a boy of fourteen. His service under Anson was therefore limited to a few months.

## Appendix V

# SERVANTS ALLOWED TO OFFICERS IN 1740

| | | |
|---|---|---|
| Admiral of the Fleet | 50 | only 16 to be borne on the books. |
| Admiral | 30 | ,, 12 ,, ,, ,, ,, ,, ,, |
| Vice-Admiral | 20 | ,, 10 ,, ,, ,, ,, ,, ,, |
| Rear-Admiral | 15 | ,, 10 ,, ,, ,, ,, ,, ,, |
| Captain | 4 | per 100 of the ship's complement |
| 1st Master ⎫<br>2nd ,, ⎪<br>Purser ⎪<br>Surgeon ⎬<br>Chaplain ⎪<br>Cook ⎭ | 1 | each in ships of 60 men or over |
| Bosn. Gunner ⎫<br>Carpenter ⎰ | 2<br>1 | each in ships of 100 men or over<br>each in ships of 60 to 100 men |

The fact that this number of servants was allowed by regulations does not mean to say they were to be found on board in every case.  Those who could be borne on the books might well be so but it was the finances of the individual officer which determined the size of his retinue.  The Captain's 'servants' usually included one or two youngsters destined for commissioned rank, a time-honoured form of entry into the service.  A number of these 'servants' might become able seamen in due course: others were tailors, barbers, footmen and fiddlers (musicians).  Commodore Edward Thompson in 1785 even had a 'painter' whom he often called up on the deck to do a sunrise or a nocturnal storm.

## Appendix VI

## CIRCUMNAVIGATORS WHO PRECEDED ANSON

| 1519 | Magellan, who did not live to see his ship reach home.  He was a Portuguese in the service of Spain. | |
|---|---|---|
| 1537 | Grijalva and Alvaradi | Spaniards |
| 1567 | Mendana | Spanish |
| 1577 | Drake | English |
| 1586 | Cavendish | English |
| 1615 | Le Maire | Dutch |
| 1625 | Quiros | Spanish |
| 1642 | Tasman | Dutch |
| 1683 | Cowley | English |
| 1689 | Dampier | English |
| 1708 | Woodes Rogers | English |
| 1719 | Clipperton | English |
| 1721 | Roggewein | Dutch |

Woodes Rogers gives details of many abortive attempts made by various mariners to sail around the world.  After Magellan had discovered the straits which are named after him, his route was the recognised one followed by ships attempting to pass from the Atlantic to the Pacific. Death, disease, mutiny and shipwreck all played their part in forcing the aspirants to return the way they had come and, for crews weakened as they mostly were by illness, the straits formed a most hazardous part of their voyage.  After the discovery in January, 1616, by Le Maire of the passage which bears his name, few mariners used the Straits of Magellan and the route round Cape Horn became the way for Pacific-bound ships.

# Appendix VII

## THE FORTUNES OF ANSON'S CREW

*The General Advertiser*, 27th July

Yesterday one Fortune, a seaman belonging to the *Centurion*, and who was on board during the whole voyage, was found dead in his bed at his lodgings in Brick Lane, Spitalfields; it is said he was very much in liquor when he went to bed.

and from the same newspaper, 23rd August:

On Tuesday night last about eleven o'clock some of the New Gentlemen belonging to the *Centurion*, having been through the City upon a frolic, attended with a fiddle and a French horn, in their return by Aldgate watch-house, fell upon one of the watchmen, and beat him very much; but some other watchmen sallying out to his assistance, the foremost man gave the word *Centurion*, upon which several more of the gang appeared and attacked them with their bludgeons and cutlasses, by which one man, whose name is Adam Parker, has got his skull broke, James Sparke two desperate wounds in the head, and—Dashley a deep and dangerous cut in the hand; several more were slightly wounded, but the damage done to lamps, lanthorns and windows is very considerable. The poor fellows were immediately carried to London Infirmary where the utmost care is taken of them. The lives of two of them, who were so terribly wounded in the head, are despaired of. It is a great pity that men should be so elevated with success as to break out into such unreasonable fits of mirth and jollity to the prejudice of quiet and peaceable people; but it will be a much greater pity and of very ill consequence, if actions like these are suffered to pass with impunity.

*Daily Post*, 22nd September

Yesterday morning a man dressed in a sailor's habit was found drowned at Lambeth, who on examination proved to be one Martin that came home in the *Centurion* with Commodore Anson. 'Tis supposed this accident happened by his being in liquor. Fifteen guineas and some silver were found in his pocket.

and on 8th November the same paper:

On Tuesday night about seven o'clock one Burton, a sailor belonging to the *Centurion* man-o-war, was attacked by four fellows between Stratford and Bow. He drew his hanger and defended himself for some time, but being overpowered they robbed him of eleven moidoires and some silver. The poor fellow received so dangerous a wound in his side that 'tis thought he will not recover.

# *Index*

## I. GENERAL

## III. PEOPLE

## IV. SHIPS